Bible Crosswords
for Kids

Collection #2

Crosswords Created and Illustrated by
Kathy Arbuckle

BIBLE CROSSWORDS FOR KIDS COLLECTION #2

EXCLUSIVE DISTRIBUTION BY PARADISE PRESS, INC.

ISBN 1-55748-726-X

30401

ADAM & EVE

GENESIS 2:15 - 3:24

ACROSS

1) THE _____ GUARDED THE GATE TO THE GARDEN.
2) IN SHAME, ADAM AND EVE _____ FROM GOD.
3) _____ WAS SECOND TO EAT THE FORBIDDEN FRUIT.
4) AFTER SINNING, ADAM AND EVE WERE SENT ___ OF THE GARDEN.
5) THE _____ TEMPTED EVE TO EAT THE FRUIT (SNAKE).

DOWN

1) ADAM NAMED THE _____.
3) EVE _____ THE FORBIDDEN FRUIT.
6) ADAM AND EVE WERE NOT TO EAT THE _____ OF THE TREE IN THE MIDDLE OF THE GARDEN.
7) THE SERPENT _____ TO EVE (DID NOT TELL THE TRUTH).

1

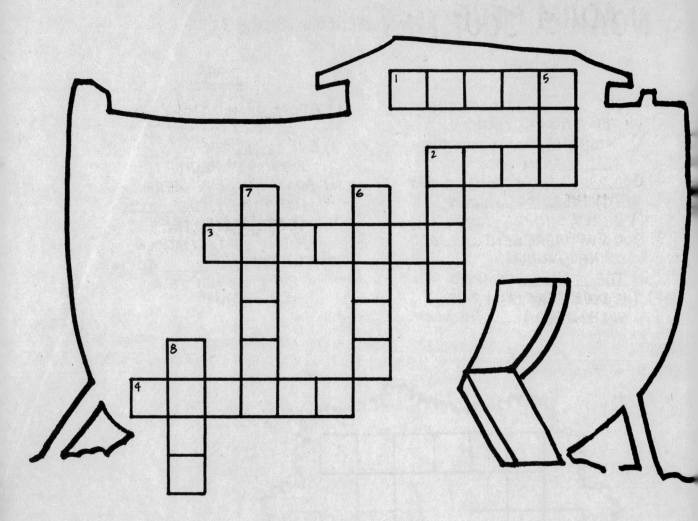

NOAH'S FAMILY BUILDS THE ARK

GENESIS 6:9-7:5

ACROSS

1) GOD SAID TO SEAL THE WOOD WITH _____.

2) NOAH'S SON

3) NOAH'S NEIGHBORS _____ AT NOAH AND HIS ARK.

4) GOD SAID TO USE THIS KIND OF WOOD TO BUILD THE ARK.

DOWN

2) NOT FRONT OR BACK, BUT _____

5) NOAH'S SON

6) THE ARK WAS _____ STORIES TALL INSIDE.

7) NOAH'S SON

8) GOD TOLD _____ HOW BIG TO BUILD THE ARK.

NOAH'S JOURNEY

GENESIS 7

ACROSS

1) WATER FALLING FROM THE SKY

2) GOD SAVED NOAH AND ALL HIS _____.

3) GOD SHUT THE _____ OF THE ARK.

4) THE DOVE CAME BACK TO NOAH WITH AN _____ BRANCH.

5) _____ COVERED ALL THE EARTH DURING THE FLOOD.

DOWN

1) GOD SET A _____ IN THE SKY AS A SIGN OF HIS PROMISE.

2) IT RAINED FOR _____ DAYS AND NIGHTS.

6) A BIRD NOAH SENT OUT FROM THE ARK – RHYMES WITH "LOVE"

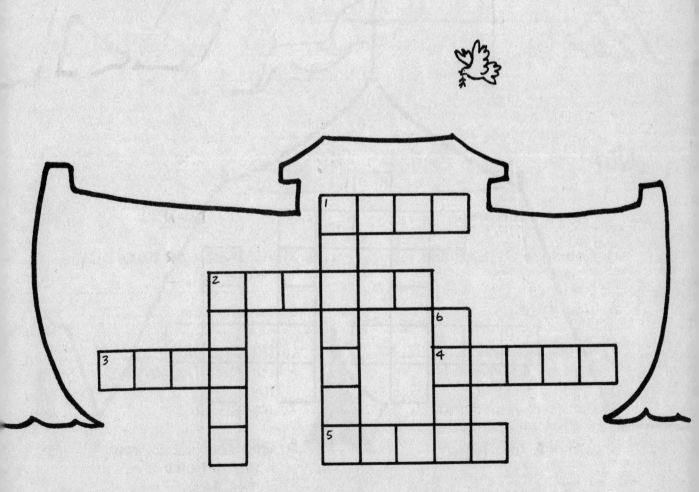

ABRAM'S JOURNEY

GENESIS 11:31 - 13:4

ACROSS

1) ABRAM'S WIFE

2) ABRAM'S FATHER

3) ABRAM AND HIS FAMILY JOURNEYED TO A FAR-AWAY ____.

DOWN

4) ABRAM LEFT THE CHALDEAN CITY OF ___.

5) SARAI'S HUSBAND.

6) FALSE GODS.

7) ABRAM'S FAMILY LIVED IN _____ FOR SHELTER AS THEY JOURNEYED.

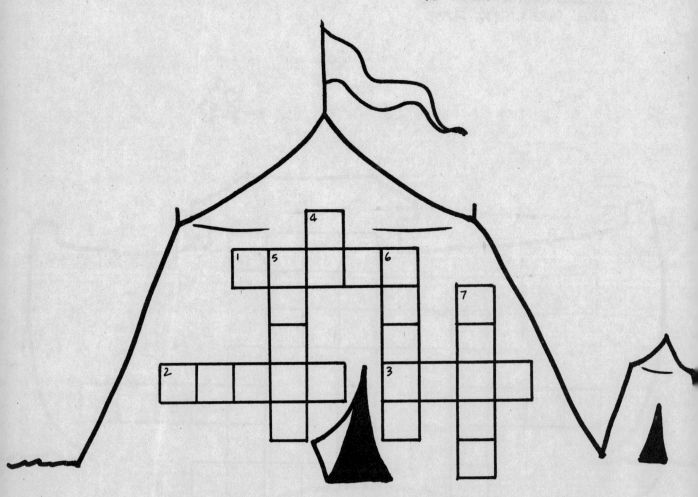

GOD'S COVENANT WITH ABRAHAM

GENESIS 15:1-18

ACROSS

1) GOD MADE A _____ TO GIVE ABRAM A SON.

2) ABRAM HAD NO _____.

DOWN

3) ABRAM LOVED ____ AND PROMISED TO SERVE HIM.

4) THE MANY LIGHTS IN THE NIGHT SKY.

5) ABRAM WAS NOW AN ____ MAN, NOT YOUNG.

6) GOD WOULD GIVE ABRAM AND SARAI A _____.

SODOM AND GOMORRAH   GENESIS 19:1-30

ACROSS

1) GOD DESTROYED SODOM AND _____.

2) FIRE RAINED DOWN WITH _____.

3) _____ AND PEPPER.

4) THE WICKED CITY WHERE LOT LIVED.

DOWN

5) LOT FLED SODOM WITH HIS WIFE AND 2 _____.

6) _____ AND BRIMSTONE RAINED DOWN TO DESTROY THE TWO CITIES.

7) LOT'S WIFE LOOKED BACK AND BECAME A _____ OF SALT.

8) ABRAHAM'S NEPHEW WHO LIVED IN SODOM.

ISAAC'S BIRTH

GENESIS 21:1-8

ACROSS

1) THE SOUND OF LAUGHING.

2) ABRAHAM AND SARAH'S SON.

3) TALK TO GOD.

DOWN

4) ABRAHAM WAS 100 WHEN ISAAC WAS BORN. SARAH WAS ALSO VERY _____.

5) ISAAC GOT BIGGER. HE _____.

6) GOD _____ HIS PROMISES.

7) ISAAC'S MOTHER.

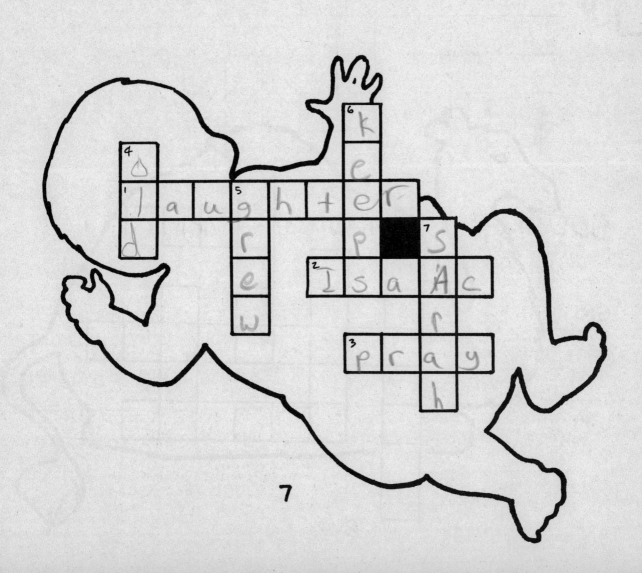

ISAAC'S BRIDE

GENESIS 24

ACROSS

1) ABRAHAM'S SERVANT GAVE REBEKAH A _____ TO WEAR ON HER FINGER...

2) ...AND 2 GOLD _____ TO WEAR ON HER WRISTS.

3) REBEKAH GAVE WATER TO THESE HUMP-BACKED ANIMALS.

DOWN

4) ISAAC'S WIFE.

5) ABRAHAM'S SON.

6) NEWLY MARRIED WOMAN. "HERE COMES THE _____."

7) REBEKAH DREW WATER FROM THE _____.

8

JACOB'S DREAM

GENESIS 28:10-16

ACROSS

1) A VISION DURING SLEEP
2) ROCK
3) GOD'S HEAVENLY MESSENGERS
4) WHAT YOU REST YOUR HEAD ON AT NIGHT AS YOU SLEEP.
5) GOD TOLD JACOB HE WOULD GIVE HIM THE _____ HE WAS LYING ON.
6) KIDS

DOWN

2) WHAT WE DO WHEN WE ARE TIRED AT NIGHT
7) HIGH DWELLING PLACE OF GOD
8) USED TO STEP UP ON TO REACH HIGH PLACES
9) FIRST-_____, BAND_____, HELP.

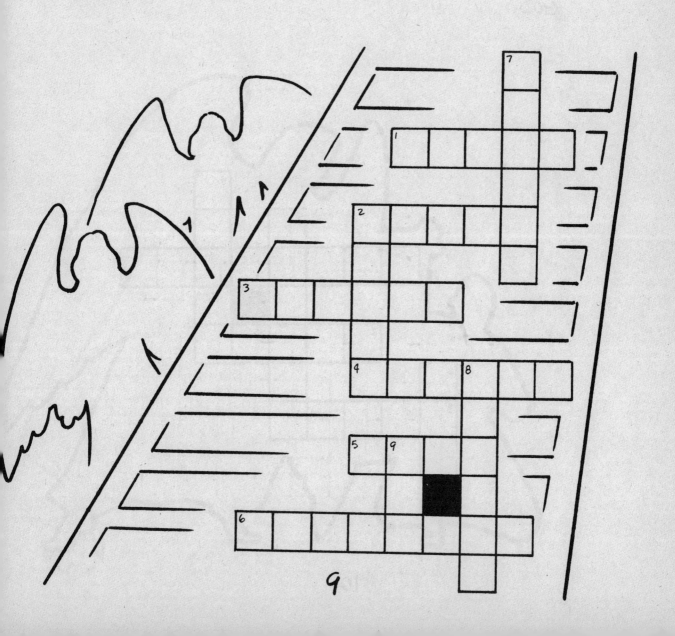

9

JACOB WRESTLES THE ANGEL

GENESIS 32:24-31

ACROSS

1) THE GRACE BEFORE A MEAL

2) TO STRETCH OUT FOR SOMETHING

3) A MESSENGER OF GOD.

DOWN

4) THE ANGEL TOUCHED JACOB'S _____.

5) JACOB'S NEW NAME

6) DAYBREAK, SUNRISE

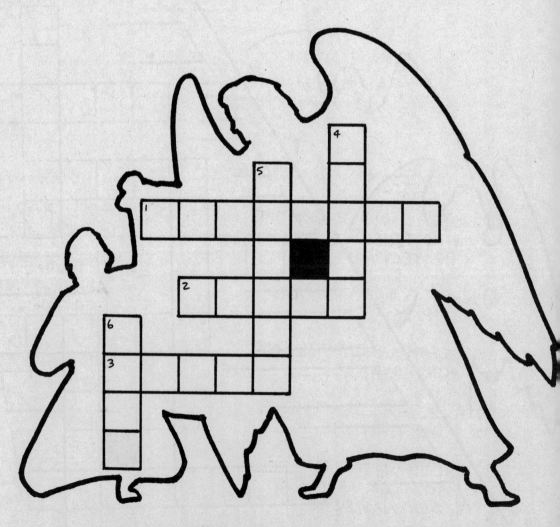

JOSEPH'S TROUBLE

GENESIS 37: 15-35

ACROSS

1) JOSEPH'S OLDER BROTHER WHO TRIED TO PROTECT HIM

2) WHAT FLOWS THROUGH OUR VEINS

3) JOSEPH'S BROTHERS SOLD HIM AS A _____.

4) A LARGE, DEEP HOLE IN THE GROUND

5) JACOB WAS VERY _____ TO HEAR THAT HIS SON WAS DEAD.

DOWN

6) JOSEPH HAD ELEVEN _____.

7) TO LET SOMETHING FALL - RHYMES WITH "CROP"

8) JOSEPH AND HIS BROTHERS TENDED THEIR FATHER'S _____ OF SHEEP.

PHARAOH'S DREAM

GENESIS 41

ACROSS

1) A VISION DURING SLEEP

2) KING OF EGYPT

3) THE NUMBER AFTER "SIX"

4) IN WHAT MANNER?
RHYMES WITH "COW"

5) OPPOSITE OF OUT

6) OVERWEIGHT

DOWN

5) NOT A HE, NOT A SHE, BUT AN ___

7) OPPOSITE OF POOR

8) OPPOSITE OF QUESTION

9) UNDERWEIGHT
RHYMES WITH "PIN"

10) A CEREAL CROP, SUCH
AS WHEAT. RHYMES
WITH "TRAIN"

11) PLURAL OF FEMALE
CATTLE

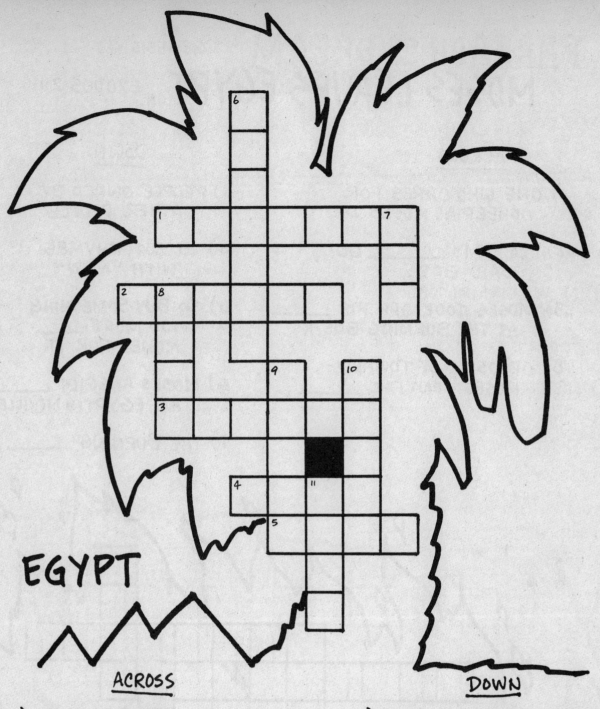

EGYPT

ACROSS

1) KING OF EGYPT

2) HUGE SCULPTURE OF A LION WITH A MAN'S FACE

3) A FALSE IMAGE OF WATER IN THE DESERT

4) THE MIGHTY _____ RIVER FLOWS THROUGH EGYPT.

5) THE DESERT HAS _____ DUNES

DOWN

6) HUGE TRIANGULAR STRUCTURE

7) OPPOSITE OF COLD

8) _____ TREE, RHYMES WITH "CALM"

9) A PLACE OF SHADE AND WATER IN THE DESERT

10) THE NUMBER AFTER SIX

11) A BABY SHEEP

MOSES LEAVES EGYPT

EXODUS 2:11

ACROSS

1) ONE WHO CARES FOR SHEEP AS MOSES DID

2) "LET MY _____ GO!", SAID GOD.

3) MOSES TOOK OFF HIS _____ AT THE BURNING BUSH.

8) OPPOSITE OF TOWARD - MOSES WENT FAR _____.

DOWN

1) PEOPLE OWNED BY OTHER PEOPLE

4) TO CUT, RHYMES WITH "NEW"

5) TO BUY SOMETHING YOU MUST _____ MONEY FOR IT.

6) MOSES ANGRILY _____ AN EGYPTIAN (KILLED).

7) THE BURNING _____

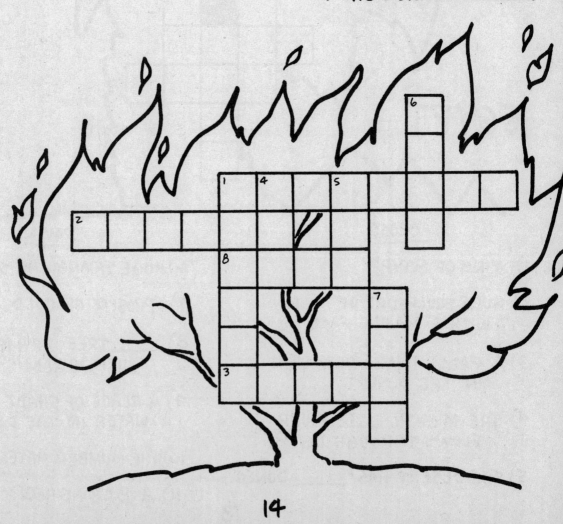

14

PASSOVER

EXODUS 12:1-36

ACROSS

1) A BABY SHEEP
2) THE ISRAELITES LEFT EGYPT QUICKLY, IN _____.
3) THEY ATE _____ HERBS WITH THEIR PASSOVER MEAL.
4) ONE TIME
5) THE ISRAELITES PUT _____ ON THEIR DOORPOSTS AS A SIGN FOR DEATH TO PASS BY THAT HOUSE.

DOWN

6) GOD SPARED THE FIRST-BORN OF THE HEBREWS ON THE NIGHT OF _____.
7) THE ISRAELITES ATE UNLEAVENED _____.
8) YOU MUST _____ RAW MEAT. RHYMES WITH "BOOK"

THE RED SEA

EXODUS 14

ACROSS

1) TWO-WHEELED WAR WAGONS DRAWN BY SWIFT HORSES

2) THE PEOPLE CROSSED THE RED SEA ON _____ LAND.

3) GOD _____ THE ISRAELITES FROM PHARAOH. RHYMES WITH "PAVED"

DOWN

4) PHARAOH'S GREAT _____ OF MEN AND CHARIOTS WAS DESTROYED.

5) THE RED _____

6) WALLS OF _____ WERE ON BOTH SIDES OF THE PEOPLE AS THEY CROSSED THE SEA ON DRY LAND.

WATER FROM THE ROCK

EXODUS 17:1-7

ACROSS

1) GOD TOLD MOSES TO _____ THE ROCK. RHYMES WITH "PIT"

2) THE MAN GOD CHOSE TO LEAD HIS PEOPLE FROM EGYPT

3) IF YOU ARE THIRSTY, HAVE SOMETHING TO _____.

4) OPPOSITE OF IN

DOWN

5) GOD'S PEOPLE WERE _____ WITHOUT WATER TO DRINK

6) WATER CAME OUT OF THE _____ AFTER MOSES HIT IT.

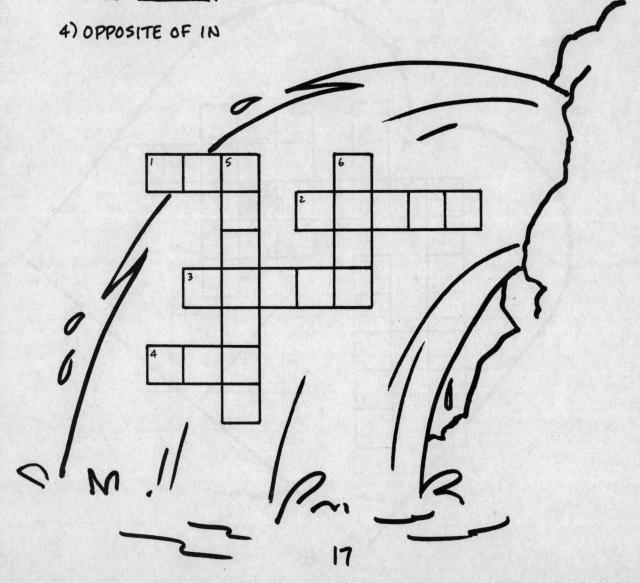

17

THE TEN COMMANDMENTS EXODUS 20:1-17

ACROSS

1) FALSE GODS

2) TO TAKE FROM SOMEONE
   WITHOUT PERMISSION

3) OPPOSITE OF TRUTH

4) DO NOT USE GOD'S
   NAME IN ____.
   (RHYMES WITH "RAIN")

DOWN

2) KEEP THE _____ DAY

5) THERE IS ONLY ___ GOD.

6) "THOU SHALL NOT ____."

7) "THOU SHALL NOT _____
    THY NEIGHBOR'S GOODS."

8) "_____ THY MOTHER AND
    FATHER."

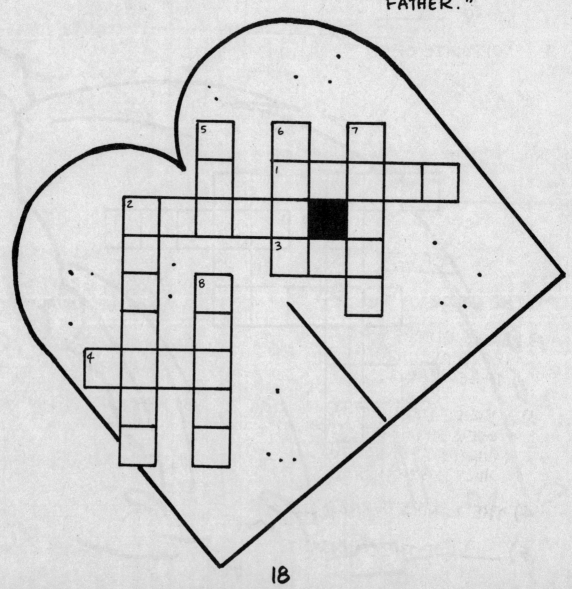

THE TABERNACLE

EXODUS 25,26

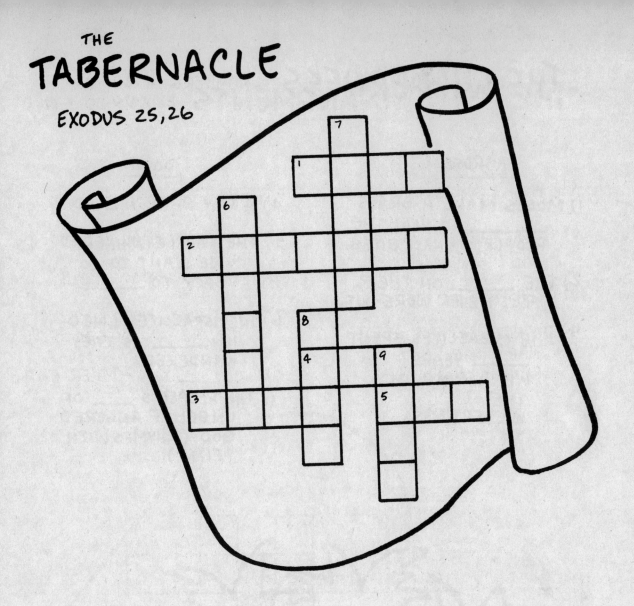

ACROSS

1) THE COLOR OF THE SKY

2) LARGE PIECES OF CLOTH HUNG AROUND THE TABERNACLE

3) A BRIDE WEARS THIS OVER HER FACE, THE CURTAIN BEFORE THE HOLY OF HOLIES.

4) THE LAMPS BURNED ____.

5) ____ OF THE COVENANT

DOWN

6) COLOR OF GRAPE SODA COLOR OF ROYALTY

7) SACRIFICES WERE BURNED ON AN ____.

8) PRECIOUS YELLOW METAL

9) BURNS OIL FOR LIGHT

THE WILDERNESS

NUMBERS 14:20-24

ACROSS

1) MOSES MADE A BRASS _____ TO HEAL THE PEOPLE'S SNAKE BITES.

2) THE _____ ON THEIR FEET NEVER WORE OUT.

3) THE ISRAELITES SPENT _____ YEARS WANDERING IN THE WILDERNESS.

DOWN

4) A DRY BARREN LAND

5) THE PEOPLE WHINED, "WE WANT TO GO BACK TO _____."

6) THE ISRAELITES LIVED IN _____ AS THEY WANDERED.

7) THE PEOPLE'S _____ OF UNBELIEF ANGERED GOD. (RHYMES WITH "FIN")

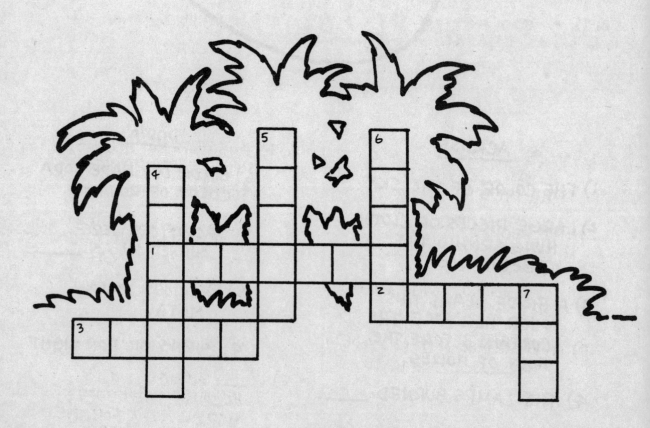

THE PROMISED LAND
DEUTERONOMY 34

ACROSS

1) MOSES WAS 120 YEARS _____ WHEN HE DIED.

2) THE PEOPLE HAD TO CROSS THE _____ RIVER TO ENTER CANAAN. (STARTS WITH J, ENDS WITH N)

3) A BASEBALL MIT IS MADE TO _____ THE BALL.

DOWN

3) MOSES WAS NOT ALLOWED TO _____ THE RIVER JORDAN.

4) MOSES _____ BEFORE THE PEOPLE ENTERED THE PROMISED LAND (PASSED AWAY).

5) THE LAND WAS FLOWING WITH MILK AND _____.

6) _____ BURIED MOSES BECAUSE THE PEOPLE HAD ALL LEFT FOR THE PROMISED LAND.

THE SPIES

JOSHUA 2

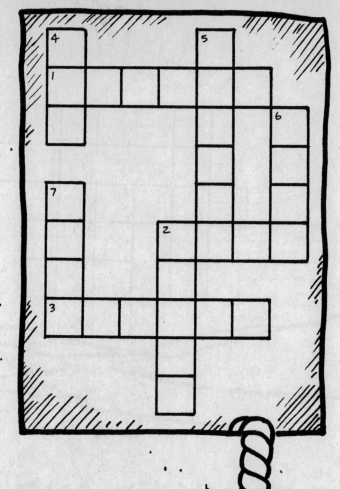

ACROSS

1) AN OPENING IN THE WALL
   TO THE OUTSIDE

2) THE SPIES PROMISED TO
   KEEP RAHAB'S FAMILY
   _____ FROM HARM.

3) RELATIVES

DOWN

2) SECRET AGENTS (RHYMES WITH "FLIES")

4) THE NUMBER THAT COMES AFTER "ONE"

5) GOD PUT _____ IN CHARGE OF THE
   PEOPLE AFTER MOSES DIED.

6) RAHAB PUT A LONG, RED _____ OUT
   HER WINDOW FOR THE SPIES TO
   CLIMB DOWN TO SAFETY.

7) THE TOP OF A HOUSE

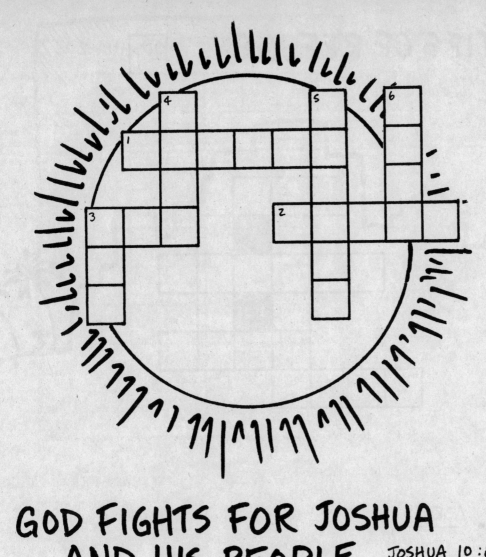

GOD FIGHTS FOR JOSHUA AND HIS PEOPLE

JOSHUA 10:8-14

ACROSS

1) THE MAN WHO LED ISRAEL AFTER MOSES DIED

2) THE SUN STOOD ———, NOT MOVING.

3) THE "LIGHT HOLDER" OF DAYTIME (RHYMES WITH "RUN")

DOWN

3) THE SPACE HIGH OVER HEAD - RHYMES WITH "PIE"

4) "LIGHT HOLDER" OF THE NIGHT (RHYMES WITH "SOON")

5) A FIGHT BETWEEN ARMIES

6) CHUNKS OF ICE FALLING FROM THE SKY LIKE RAIN

CITIES OF REFUGE

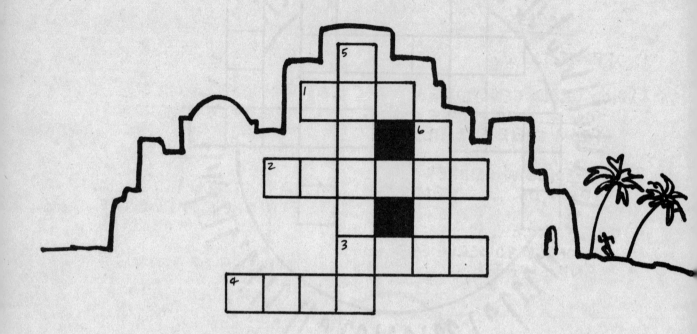

ACROSS

1) OPPOSITE OF LIVE
   RHYMES WITH "TIE"

2) LARGE TOWNS

3) TO TAKE A LIFE

4) PROTECTED FROM
   HARM

DOWN

5) AN ERROR

6) "ALIVE AND ____"
   RHYMES WITH
   "SELL"

JUDGES

ACROSS

1) OPPOSITE OF UP

2) GOD WOULD SEND JUDGES TO _____ HIS PEOPLE FROM THEIR ENEMIES.

3) THE PEOPLE WORSHIPED IDOLS, OR _____ GODS.

4) THE PEOPLE _____ THEIR PROMISE TO SERVE GOD AND SINNED.

DOWN

5) PLURAL OF JUDGE

6) THE PEOPLE WOULD _____ DOWN BEFORE IDOLS.

7) OPPOSITE OF YES

8) THE PEOPLE DID _____ IN THE SIGHT OF THE LORD. (WICKEDNESS)

9) OPPOSITE OF STRONG

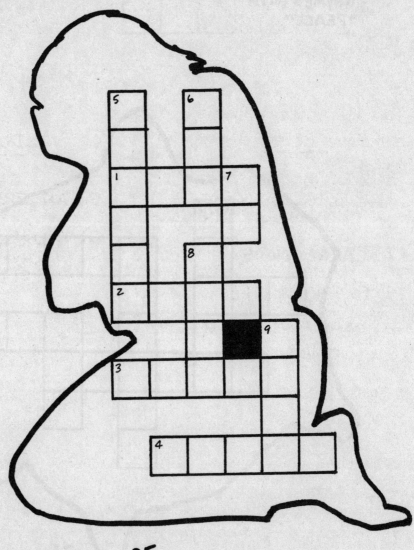

25

GIDEON

JUDGES 6

ACROSS

1) ANIMALS THAT GRAZE EAT GREEN _____.

2) AN ANGEL SPOKE TO GIDEON FROM UNDER A ____ OAK TREE. (OPPOSITE OF SMALL)

3) OPPOSITE OF WET

4) SHEEPSKIN, WOOL – RHYMES WITH "PEACE"

DOWN

1) GOD CHOSE _____ TO SAVE HIS PEOPLE FROM THE MIDIANITES.

3) WATER DROPLETS ON GRASS IN THE MORNING

5) MESSENGER OF GOD

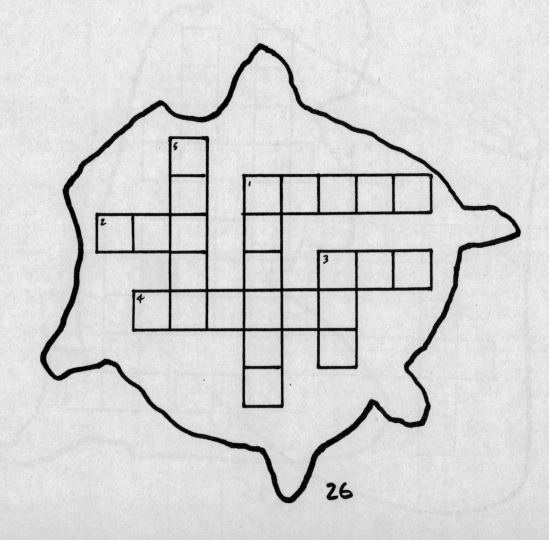

YOUNG SAMSON

JUDGES 13

ACROSS

1) BOY CHILD - RHYMES WITH "FUN"

2) KIDS

3) HIS LONG HAIR GAVE HIM HIS STRENGTH

DOWN

4) GOD'S MESSENGER

5) TO CUT A LITTLE - RHYMES WITH "BRIM"

6) TO SWALLOW A LIQUID

7) SAMSON'S _____ GREW LONG.

RUTH

ACROSS

1) BOAZ MARRIED RUTH AND SHE BECAME HIS _____.

2) RUTH _____ HER MOTHER-IN-LAW, NAOMI, WITH HER WHOLE HEART.

3) _____ FELL IN LOVE WITH RUTH AND MARRIED HER.

4) OPPOSITE OF OUT

DOWN

1) AN OWL ASKS, "_____?".

2) RUTH PROMISED TO NEVER _____ NAOMI.

4) RUTH'S MOTHER-IN-LAW

5) BOAZ LET RUTH GATHER GRAIN IN HIS MANY _____.

6) OPPOSITE OF BEGIN

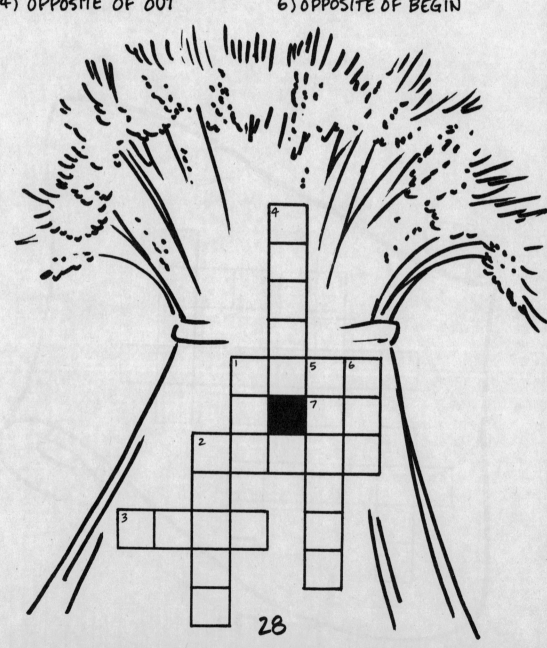

28

YOUNG SAMUEL
AND ELI

1 SAMUEL 1:24 – 2:21

ACROSS

1) SAMUEL HAD 3 BROTHERS AND 2 _____.

2) 365 DAYS

7) WHAT A CAT SAYS

DOWN

3) THE PRIEST WHO TOOK CARE OF SAMUEL

4) A JACKET

5) SAMUEL GOT BIGGER, HE _____.

6) HANNAH'S FIRST SON

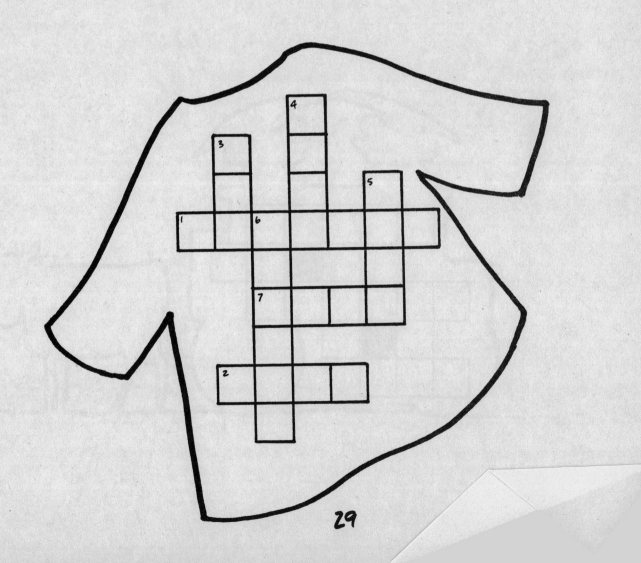

THE ARK STOLEN!   I SAMUEL 4-6

ACROSS

1) A LARGE CART PULLED BY ANIMALS

2) LARGE, STRONG CATTLE

3) TO BE FULL OF FEAR

4) _____ OF THE COVENANT

DOWN

5) HAPPY - RHYMES WITH "PLAID"

6) TO MOVE THE HEAD UP AND DOWN, RHYMES WITH "GOD"

7) NOT CLOSE - RHYMES WITH "CAR"

SAUL, A KING FOR ISRAEL

I SAMUEL 8-10

ACROSS

1) SAM IS SHORT FOR THE NAME _____.

2) YOU MAKE A SANDWICH WITH TWO SLICES OF _____.

3) A MALE RULER OF A COUNTRY. SAUL WAS ISRAEL'S FIRST ____.

DOWN

1) THE MEN ____ A SONG WITH THEIR VOICES.

4) OPPOSITE OF UNDER

5) SAMUEL POURED OIL ON TOP OF SAUL'S ____ TO ANOINT HIM.

6) ISRAEL'S FIRST KING

7) THEY BURNED ____ IN THEIR LAMPS.

31

YOUNG DAVID

1 SAMUEL 16

ACROSS

1) DAVID PLAYED _____ ON HIS HARP. (RHYMES WITH "THONGS")

2) DAVID HAD HOW MANY BROTHERS? (THE NUMBER AFTER SIX)

3) OPPOSITE OF STOP

4) THE STRINGED INSTRUMENT THAT DAVID PLAYED

5) SAMUEL POURED _____ ON DAVID'S HEAD TO ANOINT HIM.

DOWN

6) OPPOSITE OF OLD

7) DAVID WAS A SHEPHERD OVER HIS FATHER'S FLOCK OF _____.

8) DAVID WOULD PLAY SOOTHING MUSIC FOR KING _____.

9) GOD CHOSE _____ TO BE KING AFTER SAUL.

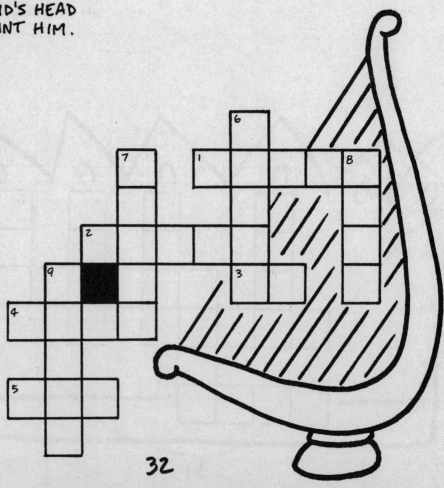

DAVID AND JONATHAN

I SAMUEL 18:1-4

ACROSS

1) _____ AND ARROW

2) SAUL'S SON

3) JONATHAN AND DAVID WERE BEST _____.

4) JONATHAN'S FATHER

DOWN

1) DAVID AND JONATHAN LOVED EACH OTHER AS IF THEY WERE _____.

5) MEN SHAKE _____ WHEN THEY FIRST MEET. (RHYMES WITH "SANDS")

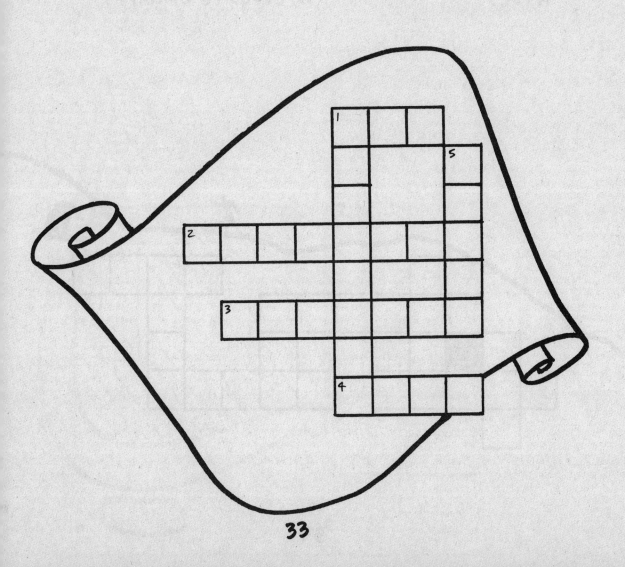

DAVID FLEES SAUL   1 SAMUEL 19

ACROSS

1) KING _____ WAS ANGRY WITH DAVID

2) OPPOSITE OF SWEET

3) OPPOSITE OF LOVED

4) SAUL BECAME AN _____ OF DAVID'S, A FOE.

DOWN

5) "_____ AND SEEK"

6) DAVID TRIED TO GET FAR _____ FROM ANGRY SAUL.

7) DAVID _____ AWAY FROM KING SAUL

8) OPPOSITE OF HAPPY

KING DAVID

2 SAMUEL 5:1-5

ACROSS

1) DAVID BECAME KING AFTER KING _____ DIED.

2) DAVID CRIED WHEN HE HEARD OF THE DEATH OF HIS BEST _____, JONATHAN.

3) HOW MANY TRIBES IN THE NATION OF ISRAEL?

4) NOW ISRAEL WOULD BE RULED BY _____, THE NEW KING.

DOWN

1) OPPOSITE OF HAPPY

5) A KING WEARS THIS ON HIS HEAD.

6) OPPOSITE OF BEGIN

7) A MAN WHO RULES OVER A COUNTRY (RHYMES WITH "RING")

8) A DEEP HOLE IN THE GROUND WHERE WATER CAN BE DRAWN.

DAVID BRINGS PEACE
2 SAMUEL 8,9

ACROSS

1) OPPOSITE OF SAD

2) LONG BATTLES BETWEEN NATIONS

3) A BUILDING THAT PEOPLE LIVE IN (RHYMES WITH "MOUSE")

4) OPPOSITE OF DOWN

DOWN

5) NO WARS OR FIGHTING

6) DAVID WAS VICTORIOUS AND ____ THE WARS HE FOUGHT.

7) DAVID TOOK CARE OF JONATHAN'S SON, AS HE PROMISED KING ____ THAT HE WOULD (RHYMES WITH "PAUL").

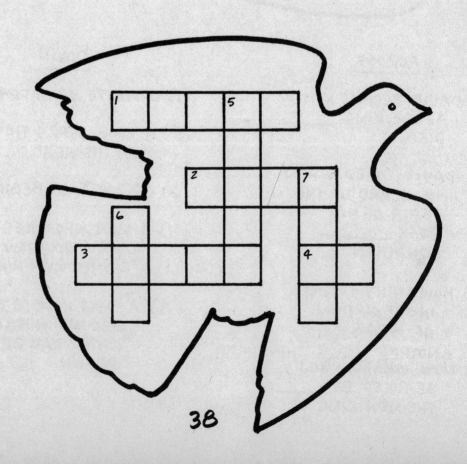

DAVID AGAIN MUST RUN

ACROSS

1) KING _____ WAS FORCED
   TO LEAVE JERUSALEM.

2) DAVID'S MEN OF WAR,
   OR _____, LEFT
   WITH HIM.

3) RIPPED, SHREDDED

4) HUSBANDS AND _____

DOWN

1) DRY, BARREN

2) OPPOSITE O

5) DAVID'S S
   MADE
   RULER

6) PEOPLE
   IN DAV

7) DAVID
   TO __

DAVID'S SON, ABSALOM, DIES

2 SAMUEL 18

<u>ACROSS</u>

1) A STAND OF MANY TREES

2) DAVID'S ARMY WAS VICTORIOUS. THEY ____ THE BATTLE.

3) WEPT

4) ABSALOM'S HAIR WAS VERY ____, NOT SHORT.

<u>DOWN</u>

5) DAVID COULD SEE THE MESSENGERS ____ QUICKLY TOWARDS HIM.

6) ABSALOM GOT HIS HAIR CAUGHT IN THE BRANCHES OF A ____.

DAVID'S LAST YEARS

ACROSS

1) WE _____ ON CHAIRS

2) NUMERAL, SUCH AS _____ ONE. (RHYMES WITH "LUMBER")

3) ROCK

4) KING DAVID WORSHIPED _____ AND LOVED HIM.

DOWN

5) SACRIFICES WOULD BE OFFERED ON AN _____.

6) DAVID ORDERED HIS HELPERS TO _____ HOW MANY MEN WERE IN ISRAEL.

7) OPPOSITE OF YOUNG

KING SOLOMON   I KINGS 2:1-11

ACROSS

1) THE NATION SOLOMON RULED OVER

2) A KING _____ ON HIS THRONE (RHYMES WITH "FITS").

3) SOLOMON WAS A _____ MAN, NOT OLD.

DOWN

4) DAVID _____ SOON AFTER SOLOMON WAS MADE KING. (OPPOSITE OF LIVED)

5) THE NUMBER AFTER NINETEEN

6) OPPOSITE OF WOMAN

7) SOLOMON WAS DAVID AND BATHSHEBA'S _____.

ONE BABY TWO MOTHERS

1 KINGS 3:16-28

ACROSS

1) TO DIVIDE SOMETHING USING A SHARP BLADE - RHYMES WITH "HUT"

2) TO BE VERY WISE IS TO HAVE _____.

3) TO CUT INTO PIECES - RHYMES WITH "ASIDE"

4) OPPOSITE OF FROM

DOWN

1) OFFSPRING - RHYMES WITH "WILD"

5) THE NUMBER AFTER THE NUMBER ONE

6) WHEN SOMETHING IS BOUGHT, IT IS _____ (RHYMES WITH "GOLD").

7) OPPOSITE OF MOTHER

8) OPPOSITE OF OUT

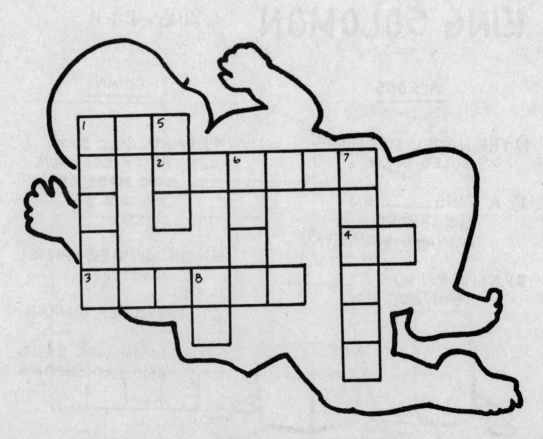

QUEEN OF SHEBA

1 KINGS 10:1-13

ACROSS

1) QUEEN OF _____

2) A HUMP-BACKED DESERT ANIMAL

3) OPPOSITE OF OLD

4) PRECIOUS YELLOW METAL

5) WEALTHY

DOWN

1) _____ WAS FULL OF WISDOM.

6) THE _____ OF SHEBA VISITED SOLOMON.

7) THE QUEEN OF SHEBA CAME FROM A _____ AWAY LAND

8) RICHES

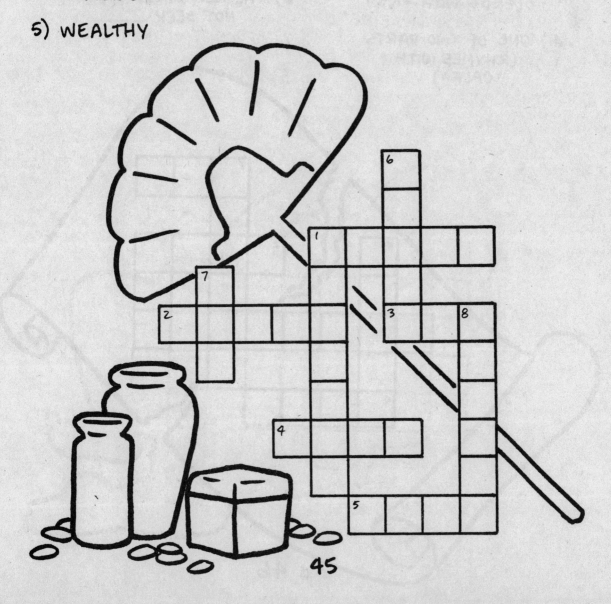

45

THE KINGDOM DIVIDES
ISRAEL & JUDAH

1 KINGS 12:16-33

ACROSS

1) THE NUMBER THAT FOLLOWS AFTER NINE

2) A MAN WHO RULES A COUNTRY

3) COUNSEL GIVEN TO HELP SOMEONE MAKE A DECISION (ENDS WITH -ICE)

4) ONE OF TWO PARTS (RHYMES WITH "CALF")

DOWN

1) ISRAEL DIVIDED ITS TWELVE _____ INTO TWO KINGDOMS.

5) THE KINGDOM WAS DIVIDED INTO ISRAEL AND _____.

6) THE NEW KINGS DID NOT SEEK _____.

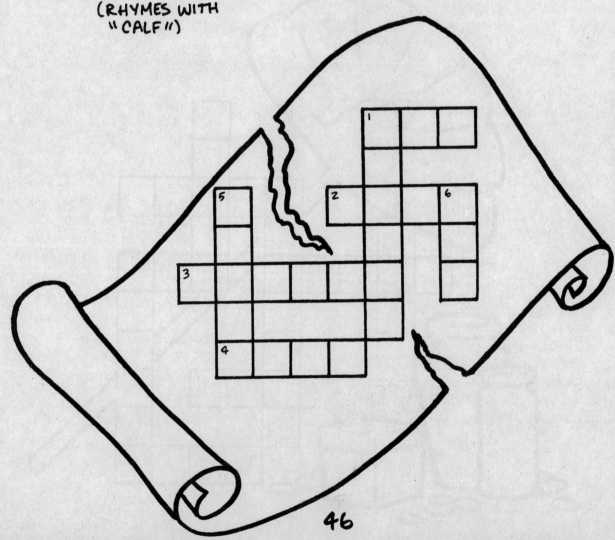

ELIJAH RAISES THE WIDOW'S SON

ACROSS

1) OPPOSITE OF LAST

2) A WOMAN WHOSE HUSBAND HAS DIED

3) TO TALK TO GOD

DOWN

1) GRAIN GROUND TO A POWDER - RHYMES WITH "HOUR"

4) LAMPS BURN _____ FOR LIGHT.

5) ILL, AILING

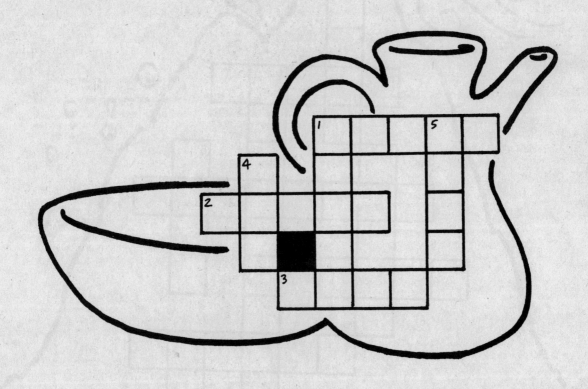

ELIJAH FLEES JEZEBEL 1 KINGS 19:1-18

ACROSS

1) A MESSENGER OF GOD

2) TALL PEAK ON THE LAND

3) STONE

4) FIRE - RHYMES WITH "GAMES"

DOWN

5) TO SWALLOW A LIQUID

6) WHEN THE GROUND SHAKES

7) YOU SPEAK WITH YOUR _____ (RHYMES WITH "CHOICE").

8) THE MOVEMENT OF AIR - RHYMES WITH "PINNED"

9) TO CONSUME FOOD

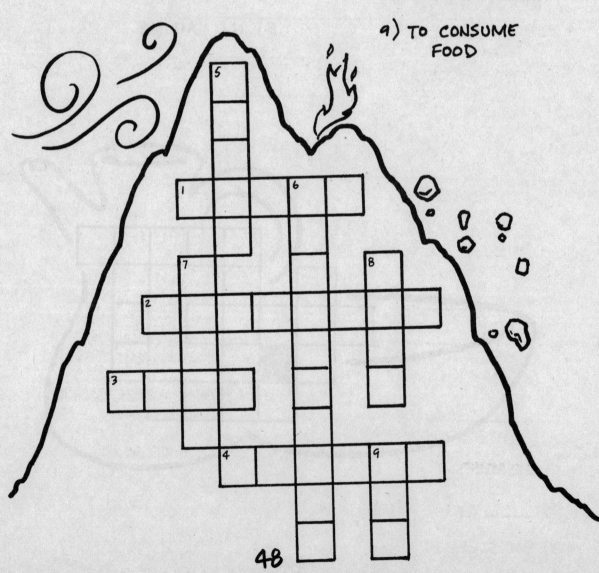

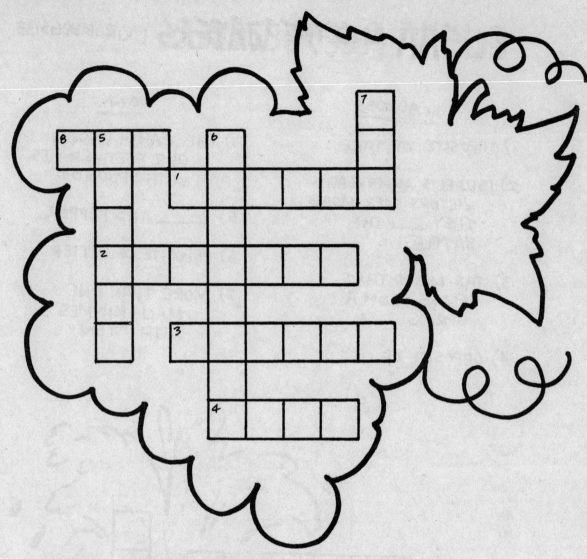

EVIL JEZEBEL   1 KINGS 21

ACROSS

1) JEZEBEL _____ THE VINEYARD'S OWNER (TOOK HIS LIFE).

2) _____ WAS A WICKED WOMAN.

3) RELATIVES

4) _____ CHASE CATS.

8) YOU SLEEP IN A _____.

DOWN

5) THE PROPHET WHO THE RAVENS FED

6) A FARM WHERE GRAPES ARE GROWN

7) OPPOSITE OF GOOD

ELISHA AND THE WATERS

ACROSS

1) OPPOSITE OF TAKE

2) ISRAEL'S ARMY HAD VICTORY OVER MOAB. THEY ___ THE BATTLE.

3) THE LIQUID THAT FLOWS FROM A SPRING

4) OPPOSITE OF LIFE

DOWN

1) THE EARTH UNDER OUR FEET - RHYMES WITH "POUND"

5) ___ AND PEPPER

6) OPPOSITE OF BITTER

7) MORE THAN ONE MAN - RHYMES WITH "TEN"

A BOY IS HEALED

2 KINGS 4:8-37

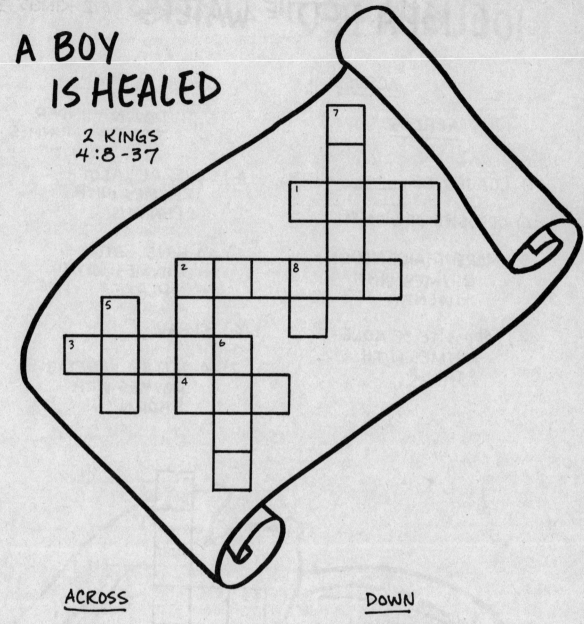

ACROSS

1) ILL

2) OPPOSITE OF MOTHER

3) THE MOTHER _____ HER BOY WITH ALL HER HEART.

4) TO BIND SOMETHING WITH STRING OR ROPE - RHYMES WITH "LIE"

DOWN

2) YOU WEAR SHOES ON THEM

5) OPPOSITE OF GIRL

6) OPPOSITE OF LIVED

7) THE BOY WAS _____ AGAIN! (OPPOSITE OF DEAD)

8) OPPOSITE OF SHE

100 MEN FED

2 KINGS 4:42-44

ACROSS

1) LOAVES OF _____

2) OPPOSITE OF WOMEN

3) MORE THAN ENOUGH -
   RHYMES WITH
   "TWENTY"

4) OPPOSITE OF NONE -
   RHYMES WITH
   "TALL"

DOWN

2) SEVERAL, ALOT -
   RHYMES WITH
   "PENNY"

5) TO HAVE EATEN
   RHYMES WITH
   "PLATE"

6) SPEAK

7) A YELLOW VEGETABLE -
   RHYMES WITH
   "HORN"

THE LOST AXHEAD 2 KINGS 6:1-7

ACROSS

1) THE AXHEAD DROPPED AND _____ INTO THE WATER (RHYMES WITH "WELL").

2) SOMETHING WOODEN IS MADE OF _____.

3) OPPOSITE OF "OUT OF"

4) CLEAR LIQUID FLOWING IN A RIVER

DOWN

1) OPPOSITE OF SINK - RHYMES WITH "BOAT"

5) OPPOSITE OF IN

6) TOOL USED FOR CHOPPING WOOD - RHYMES WITH "TAX"

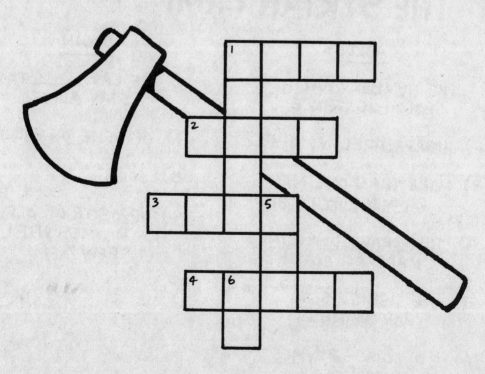

53

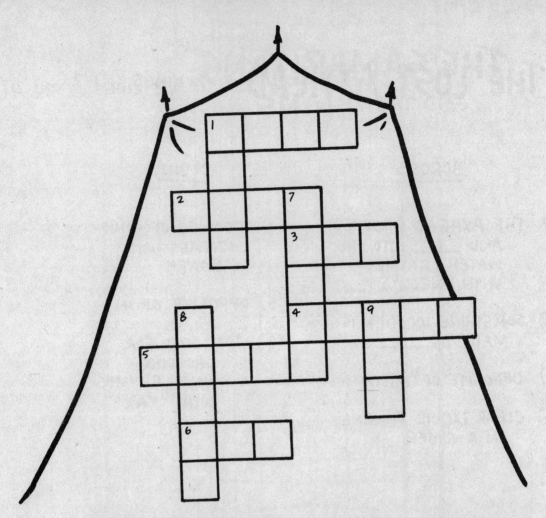

THE SYRIAN CAMP
2 KINGS 7

ACROSS

1) THE NUMBER THAT FOLLOWS THREE

2) DISAPPEARED, VANISHED

3) MORE THAN ONE MAN - RHYMES WITH "TEN"

4) TEMPORARY DWELLINGS MADE OF CLOTH

5) WE USE THIS TO BUY THINGS.

6) TO LOOK - RHYMES WITH "TEA"

DOWN

1) WE EAT _____ TO STAY ALIVE.

7) OPPOSITE OF FULL

8) SOUND

9) OPPOSITE OF OLD - RHYMES WITH "FEW"

54

THE SAMARITANS
AND THE LIONS

ACROSS

1) LARGE, MANED CATS

2) NATIONS

3) ROADS THROUGH TOWN - RHYMES WITH "TREATS"

4) LARGE TOWN

DOWN

5) FALSE GODS

6) ONLY A _____ COULD OFFER SACRIFICES OR ENTER THE TABERNACLE. (RHYMES WITH "FEAST")

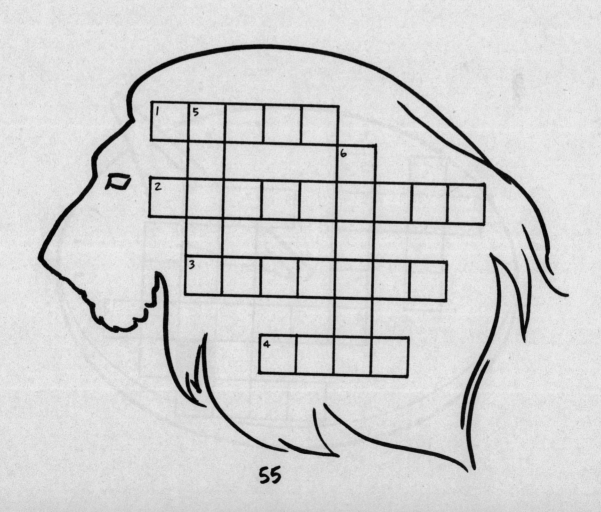

55

HEZEKIAH SPARED

2 KINGS 20:1-11

ACROSS

1) OPPOSITE OF DIE

2) A DEVICE WHICH TELLS TIME USING THE SHADOW CAST BY THE SUN

3) OPPOSITE OF UP

4) TO QUESTION— RHYMES WITH "TASK"

DOWN

5) ILL

6) WHEN WE CRY _____ FALL FROM OUR EYES.

7) THE BRIGHT SUN CASTS THE TREE'S _____ ON THE LAWN. (SHADE CAST BY AN OBJECT)

8) TALK TO GOD

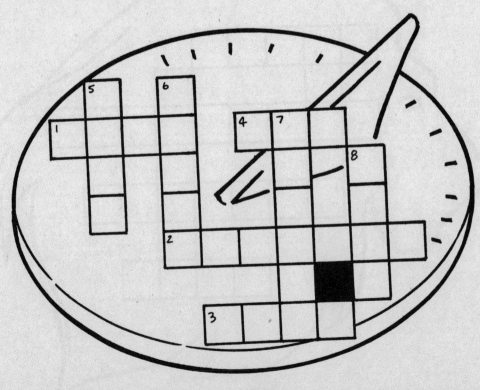

KING MANASSEH

2 KINGS 21:1-26

ACROSS

1) FALSE GODS

2) BROKE GOD'S LAW - RHYMES WITH "PINNED"

3) "LIGHT HOLDER" OF THE NIGHT SKY - RHYMES WITH "SOON"

DOWN

2) "LIGHT HOLDER" OF THE DAY - RHYMES WITH "FUN"

4) OPPOSITE OF GOOD

5) MANASSEH _____ MANY INNOCENT PEOPLE (TOOK THEIR LIVES).

6) OPPOSITE OF YES

JEHOSHAPHAT, A GOOD KING

2 CHRONICLES 20:1-21

ACROSS

1) _____ WAS A GOOD KING.

2) A MAN WHO RULES A COUNTRY

3) YOU USE A ____ TO UNLOCK A LOCK.

DOWN

4) THE PEOPLE SANG ____ OF PRAISE TO THE LORD.

5) GRATITUTE

6) JEHOSHAPHAT WOULD ____ TO GOD OFTEN, TALK TO HIM.

7) JEHOSHAPHAT LOVED GOD WITH HIS WHOLE ____.

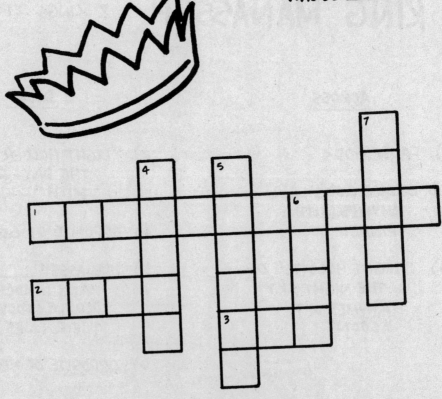

JOASH RESTORES THE TEMPLE

2 CHRONICLES 24:1-14

ACROSS

1) THE NUMBER AFTER THE NUMBER SIX

2) FIX

3) OPPOSITE OF OLD - RHYMES WITH "FEW"

4) LARGE RECTANGULAR CONTAINER - RHYMES WITH "FOX"

DOWN

5) HOUSE OF WORSHIP

6) THE BOX WAS MADE OF LUMBER, OR _____ (RHYMES WITH "GOOD").

7) OPPOSITE OF OUT

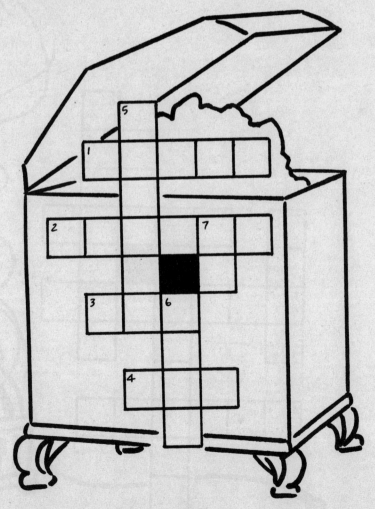

KING UZZIAH'S SIN

2 CHRONICLES 26:16-21

ACROSS

1) OPPOSITE OF OUT

2) OPPOSITE OF BEFORE

3) SERIOUS SKIN DISEASE

4) ONLY THE _____ COULD GO INTO THE HOLY PLACE TO BURN THE INCENSE.

DOWN

5) AN AROMATIC SUBSTANCE BURNED FOR FRAGRANCE

6) THE PART OF THE FACE BETWEEN THE EYEBROWS AND HAIRLINE

7) SET APART TO GOD— _____ OF HOLIES

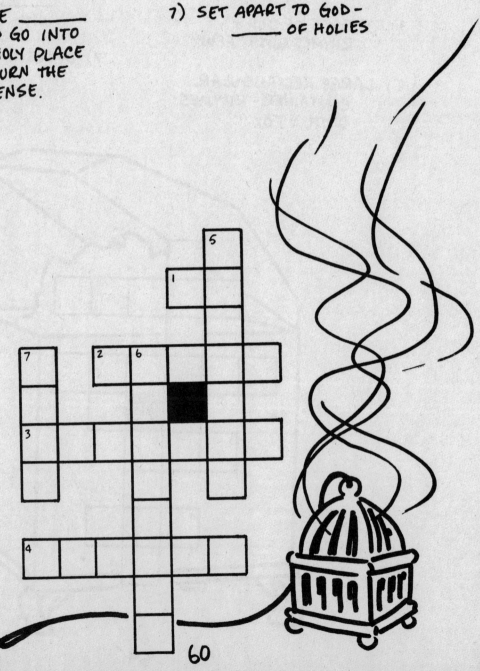

REBUILDING THE TEMPLE

EZRA 3:8-13

ACROSS

1) A STRIP OF LEATHER OR CLOTH TIED AROUND THE WAIST.

2) WEPT

3) ROCKS - RHYMES WITH "PHONES"

4) OPPOSITE OF LAST

DOWN

1) ONES WHO BUILD THINGS

5) HAPPY, JOYFUL - RHYMES WITH "HAD"

6) WE _____ ON CHAIRS - RHYMES WITH HIT

THE TEMPLE FINISHED

EZRA 6:13-18

ACROSS

1) SET APART TO GOD —
   _____ OF HOLIES

2) TO COMPLETE, TO
   GET DONE

3) THE NUMBER
   BEFORE
   THREE

DOWN

4) OPPOSITE OF BEGIN

5) THOSE WHO SPEAK FOR
   GOD — HAGGAI AND
   ZECHARIAH WERE _____.

6) HAPPINESS, GREAT GLADNESS

7) PRECIOUS YELLOW METAL

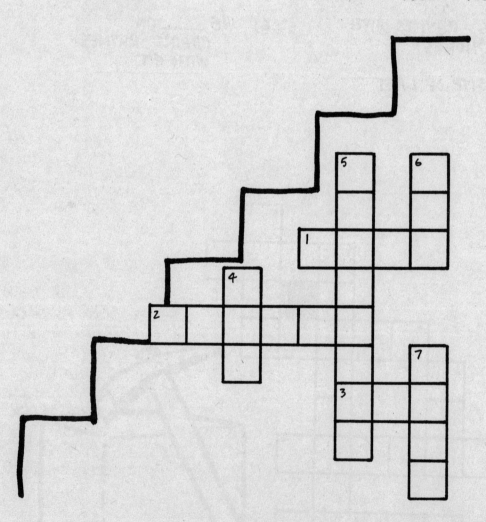

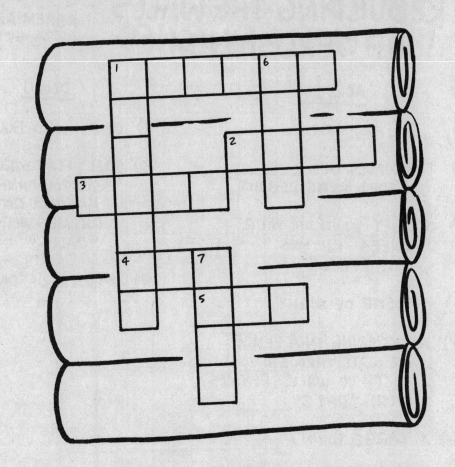

EZRA KEEPS GOD'S BOOK

EZRA

ACROSS

1) ONE WHO COPIED BOOKS AND DID THE JOB OF WRITING THINGS DOWN - RHYMES WITH "BRIBE"

2) DUPLICATE, REPRODUCTION RHYMES WITH "POPPY"

3) SET APART TO GOD - ____ OF HOLIES

4) A RULE, A STATUTE RHYMES WITH "PAW"

5) OPPOSITE OF NEW

DOWN

1) ROLLS WHICH HAVE BEEN WRITTEN ON - RHYMES WITH "ROLLS"

6) MANY PAGES BOUND TOGETHER IS A ____ - RHYMES WITH "COOK"

7) " THE ____ OF GOD " - RHYMES WITH HEARD

REBUILDING THE WALLS OF JERUSALEM

NEHEMIAH 2-5

ACROSS

1) _____ AND ARROW

2) THE WALLS OF _____ NEEDED TO BE REBUILT

3) TO GET DOWN ON YOUR KNEES - RHYMES WITH "FEEL"

4) OPPOSITE OF NIGHT

5) AN OPENING IN A FENCE OR WALL THROUGH WHICH TO WALK - RHYMES WITH "DATE"

6) A LARGE TOWN

DOWN

7) ONES WHO BUILD

8) TALL, FLAT STRUCTURES SURROUNDING ANCIENT CITIES - RHYMES WITH "CALLS"

9) OPPOSITE OF DAY

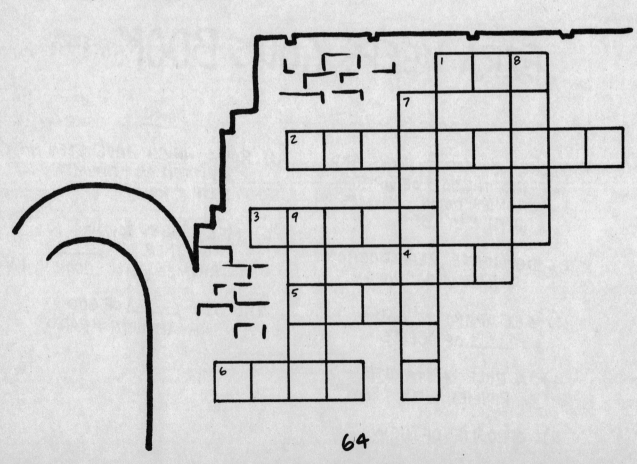

EZRA READS THE LAW

NEHEMIAH 8, 13

ACROSS

1) OPPOSITE OF PUSH

2) THE PEOPLE MADE A _____ TO GOD (A VOW).

3) _____ READ THE LAW TO THE PEOPLE.

DOWN

1) HUMAN BEINGS, NATION, RACE – RHYMES WITH "STEEPLE"

4) OPPOSITE OF SAD

5) A TALL STAND FROM WHICH A SPEAKER TALKS

6) OPPOSITE OF WORK – RHYMES WITH "BEST"

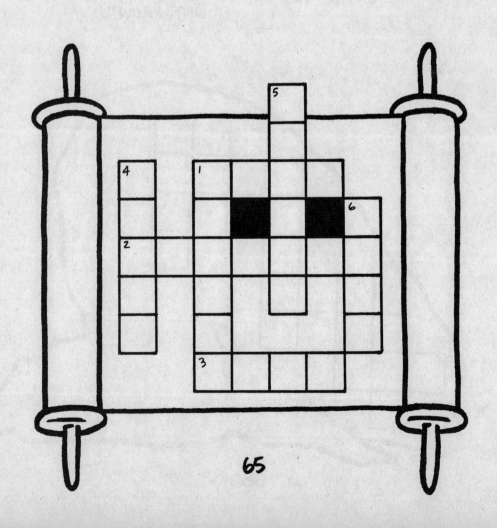

THE EVIL HAMAN

ESTHER 3

ACROSS

1) OPPOSITE OF LOVE

2) YOU WEAR A ____ ON YOUR HEAD (RHYMES WITH "CAT").

3) OPPOSITE OF UP

4) A RULE, DECREE, STATUTE - RHYMES WITH "PAW"

DOWN

1) ____ HATED THE JEWS (RHYMES WITH "CANAAN").

3) OPPOSITE OF MOM

5) MORDECAI ____ BY THE GATE EVERY DAY (RHYMES WITH "CAT").

6) CHILDREN OF ISRAEL, HEBREWS

7) HAMAN DEMANDED THAT EVERYONE ____ DOWN TO HIM (RHYMES WITH "HOW").

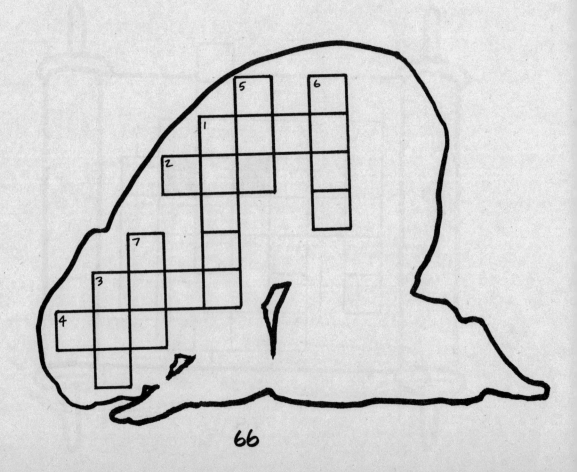

ESTHER TELLS
OF
HAMAN'S PLOT

ACROSS

1) ESTHER _____ HER PEOPLE FROM HAMAN'S EVIL PLOT (RHYMES WITH "PAVED").

2) _____ WAS GOING TO KILL THE JEWS.

3) OPPOSITE OF HIM

4) THE CHILDREN OF ISRAEL, HEBREWS

DOWN

5) GOD USED QUEEN _____ TO SAVE THE JEWS.

6) A LARGE MEAL LATER IN THE DAY - RHYMES WITH "THINNER"

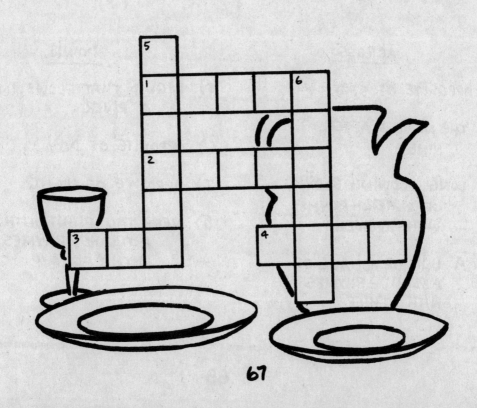

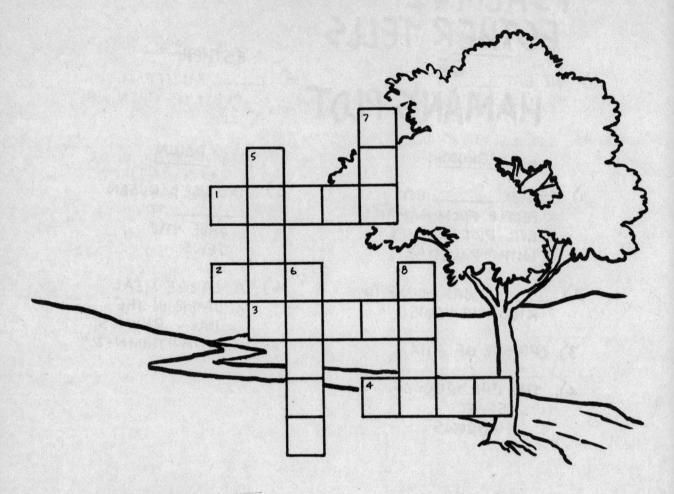

PSALM 1

ACROSS

1) OPPOSITE OF SAD

2) THE NUMBER AFTER NINE

3) LONG, FLOWING BODY OF WATER - RHYMES WITH "QUIVER"

4) A UNIT OF FOLIAGE OF A PLANT - RHYMES WITH "THIEF"

DOWN

5) LIQUID THAT FLOWS IN A RIVER

6) OPPOSITE OF DAY

7) OPPOSITE OF NIGHT

8) VERY TALL PLANT WITH A TRUNK - RHYMES WITH "FREE"

PSALM 42

ACROSS

1) WE EAT _____ TO LIVE.

2) _____ FLOWS OUT OF A FOUNTAIN.

3) WITHOUT WATER TO DRINK YOU HAVE _____ (RHYMES WITH "FIRST")

DOWN

3) _____ FALL FROM OUR EYES WHEN WE CRY.

4) WATER SHOOTING UP OR OUT - RHYMES WITH "MOUNTAIN"

5) A GRACEFUL ANIMAL WITH ANTLERS - RHYMES WITH "FEAR"

6) SMALL RIVER OR BROOK - RHYMES WITH "CREAM"

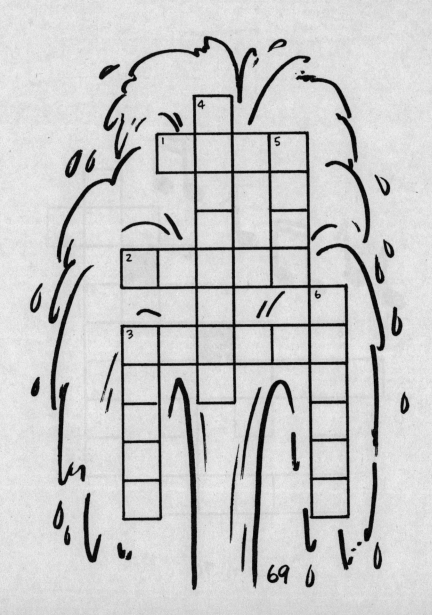

69

PSALM 117

ACROSS

1) OPPOSITE OF HERS

2) "PRAISE THE _____"

3) TO WORSHIP, ADORE, EXTOL - RHYMES WITH "RAISE"

4) "_____ THY MOTHER AND THY FATHER"

DOWN

5) BENEVOLENCE, THE QUALITY OF BEING KIND

6) ETERNITY

7) OPPOSITE OF HER

8) OPPOSITE OF LIE

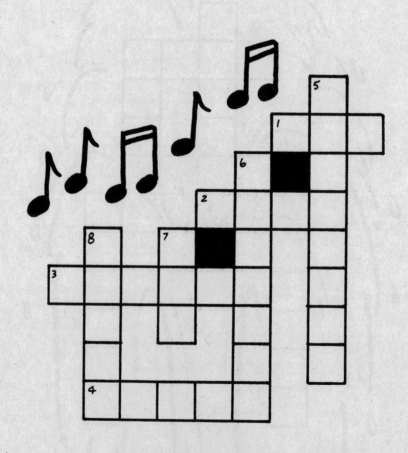

THE VIRTUOUS WOMAN

PROVERBS 31:10-31

ACROSS

1) LABORS, EFFORTS, TASKS
   RHYMES WITH "PERKS"

2) THE LIMBS THAT EXTEND
   FROM THE SHOULDERS

3) OPPOSITE OF BAD

4) "CLAP YOUR _____."
   RHYMES WITH
   "SANDS"

5) A WOMAN IS MARRIED
   TO HER _____.

DOWN

1) OPPOSITE OF MAN

4) A BUILDING
   PEOPLE LIVE IN

6) OPPOSITE OF
   WEAK

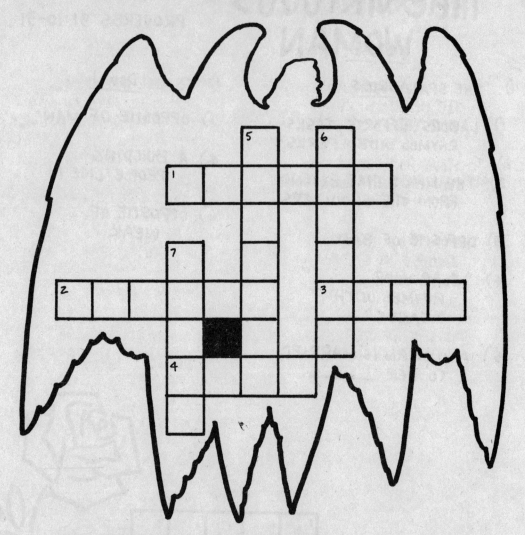

ISAIAH the PROPHET

ISAIAH 6

ACROSS

1) A KING SITS ON A _____.

2) GOD GAVE _____ A VISION OF PROPHESY.

3) WE SPEAK WITH OUR TONGUE AND ____ (RHYMES WITH "SIPS").

4) AN OPENING IN A FENCE THROUGH WHICH TO WALK - RHYMES WITH "LATE"

DOWN

5) ONE WHO SPEAKS FOR GOD; ISAIAH WAS A GREAT _____.

6) GOD'S MESSENGERS

7) BIRDS AND ANGELS USE THESE TO FLY.

THE SOARING EAGLE

Isaiah 40:31

ACROSS

1) THE SPACE OVERHEAD, THE HEAVENS - RHYMES WITH "FLY"

2) TO MOVE AS FAST AS YOU CAN BY FOOT - RHYMES WITH "FUN"

3) THE FINAL AIM IN A CONTEST, TO GET A POINT - RHYMES WITH "SOUL"

4) OPPOSITE OF WEAK

DOWN

1) TO RISE UP HIGH, "_____ LIKE AN EAGLE" - RHYMES WITH "POOR"

5) BIRDS FLAP THEIR _____.

6) THE OPPOSITE ONE OF TWO - "NOT THAT ONE. THE _____ ONE."

7) "PRAISE THE _____."

8) LARGE BIRD OF PREY, SYMBOL OF THE USA

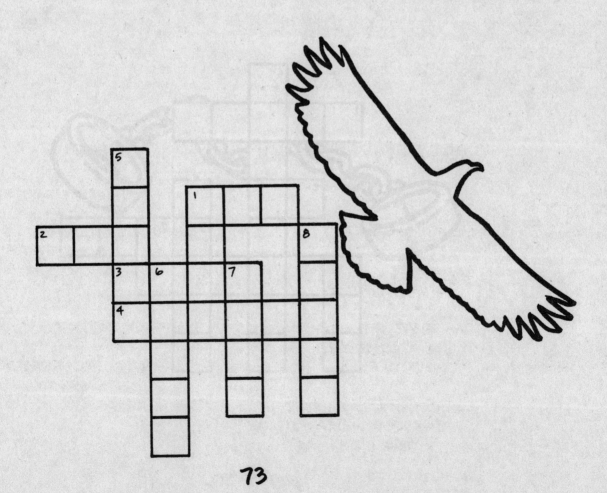

JEREMIAH IN PRISON

ACROSS

1) TO TALK, TO UTTER SPEECH - RHYMES WITH "PEAK"

2) OPPOSITE OF SHE

3) OPPOSITE OF UP

4) A PLACE WHERE PEOPLE ARE HELD CAPTIVE, A DUNGEON - RHYMES WITH "RISEN"

DOWN

4) A DEEP HOLE IN THE GROUND - RHYMES WITH "PIT"

5) _____ WAS THROWN IN PRISON.

6) FALSE GODS

7) OPPOSITE OF OFF

74

EZEKIEL'S VISION

EZEKIEL 37:1-14

ACROSS

1) OPPOSITE OF FOUND

2) THE LOWLAND BETWEEN TWO MOUNTAINS - RHYMES WITH "GALLEY"

3) ONLY A _____ COULD OFFER SACRIFICES TO THE LORD.

4) THE PARTS OF OUR SKELETON - RHYMES WITH "STONES"

DOWN

5) OPPOSITE OF DEAD

6) GOD GAVE _____ A VISION.

7) ANTICIPATION OF A GOOD THING - RHYMES WITH "SOAP"

DANIEL AND THE KING'S DREAM

ACROSS

1) YOU WEAR SHOES ON YOUR ____.

2) THE PLATE ____ WHEN I DROPPED IT.- RHYMES WITH "JOKE"

3) ____ COULD TELL THE MEANINGS OF THE KING'S DREAMS.

4) THE COLOR OF CLAY- RHYMES WITH "PLAY"

5) A PRECIOUS METAL - WE USE ____ WARE TO EAT WITH.

DOWN

4) PRECIOUS YELLOW METAL

6) ROCK

7) A VISION DURING SLEEP

8) A THICK, MOLDABLE SUBSTANCE, CAN BE FIRED TO MAKE POTTERY- RHYMES WITH "GRAY"

9) TO HAVE EATEN - RHYMES WITH "PLATE"

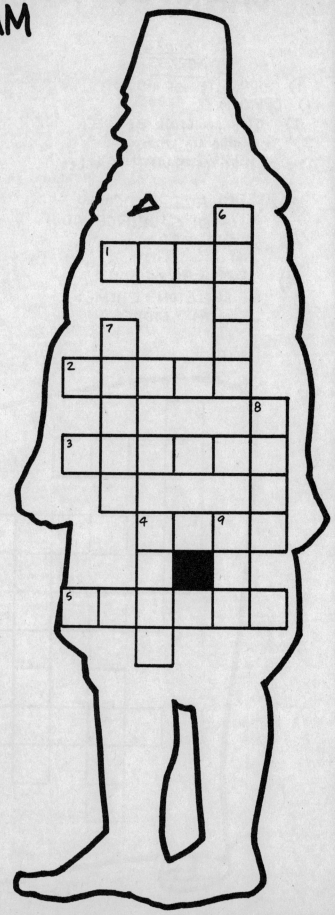

76

DANIEL AND THE LIONS

ACROSS

1) OPPOSITE OF CLOSED

2) THE LIONS DID NOT HARM _____.

3) AN OPENING THROUGH THE WALL TO THE OUTSIDE TO LET IN LIGHT AND FRESH AIR.

4) TO GET DOWN ON YOUR KNEES - RHYMES WITH "FEEL"

DOWN

5) A CAVE WHERE THE LIONS LIVED - RHYMES WITH "PEN"

6) TO TALK TO GOD

7) OPPOSITE OF MANY

8) KINGS OF BEASTS

9) A FEMALE DEER

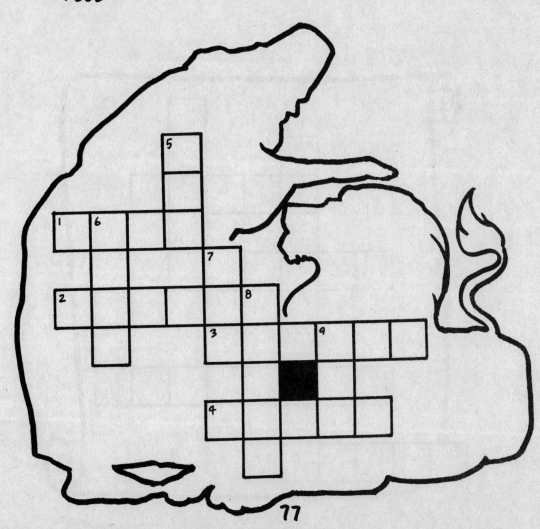

ZACHARIAS

LUKE 1:5-25

ACROSS

1) A MESSENGER OF GOD, GABRIEL, THE _____

2) _____ THE BAPTIST

3) KIDS

4) ZACHARIAS WAS A _____ WHO SERVED IN THE TEMPLE (RHYMES WITH "FEAST").

DOWN

5) FOR A TIME ZACHARIAS COULD NOT _____ (TALK).

6) AN ANGEL APPEARED TO _____ (JOHN THE BAPTIST'S FATHER).

7) OPPOSITE OF YOUNG

8) A BOY CHILD - RHYMES WITH "FUN" OPPOSITE OF DAUGHTER

MARY VISITS ELIZABETH LUKE 1:39-45

ACROSS

1) THE CHILD OF ONE'S UNCLE OR AUNT - RHYMES WITH "DOZEN"

2) MARY WENT TO VISIT HER COUSIN_____.

3) GLADNESS, GREAT HAPPINESS

4) ELIZABETH WOULD HAVE A _____ BOY (RHYMES WITH "MAYBE")

DOWN

5) TO GO SEE SOMEONE FOR A SHORT STAY

6) THE MOTHER OF JESUS

7) SET APART TO GOD, _____ OF HOLIES

THE ANGELS TELL THE SHEPHERDS

LUKE 2:8-20

ACROSS

1) GREAT GLADNESS, HAPPINESS

2) THOSE WHO CARE FOR SHEEP

3) "GLORY TO _____ IN THE HIGHEST"

DOWN

1) _____ WAS THE NEWBORN SAVIOR.

2) TO LOOK WITH YOUR EYES - RHYMES WITH "BEE"

4) GOD'S MESSENGERS

5) OPPOSITE OF DAY

6) FEARFUL

7) THE SPACE HIGH OVERHEAD, THE HEAVENS - RHYMES WITH "PIE"

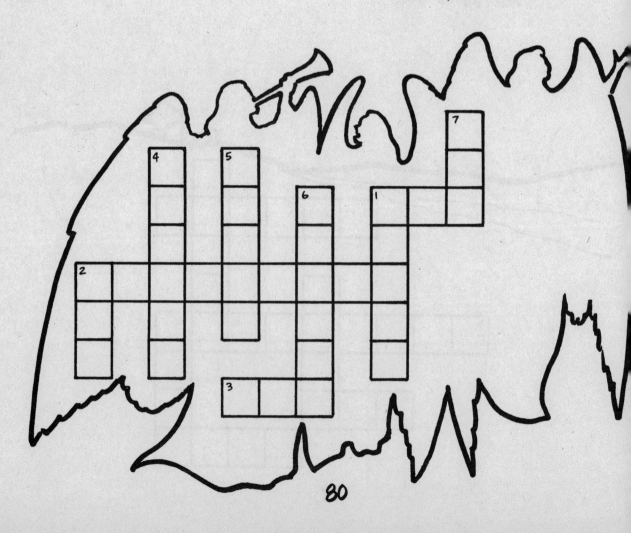

THE WISE MEN

Matthew 2:1-12

ACROSS

1) PRECIOUS YELLOW METAL

2) OPPOSITE OF WEST

3) IF YOU HAVE WISDOM, YOU ARE _____.

4) PRESENTS

5) MOTHER OF JESUS

6) THE MAN WHO RULES OVER A COUNTRY

DOWN

5) OPPOSITE OF WOMEN

7) THE BUILDING PEOPLE LIVE IN - RHYMES WITH "MOUSE"

8) HUMP-BACKED DESERT CREATURES

9) SMALL CITY - RHYMES WITH "DOWN"

10) BRIGHT POINT OF LIGHT IN THE NIGHT SKY

11) THE SPACE OVERHEAD, THE HEAVENS - RHYMES WITH "PIE"

81

JESUS AS A BOY

LUKE 2:39-40

ACROSS

1) AN ANGEL TOLD JOSEPH TO ___ BACK TO ISRAEL (OPPOSITE OF STOP).

2) IF YOU HAVE WISDOM, YOU ARE ___ (RHYMES WITH "EYES").

3) OPPOSITE OF GIRL

4) FATHER, SON, HOLY ___

DOWN

1) GOT BIGGER

3) A CREATURE WITH FEATHERS AND WINGS

5) THE SON OF GOD

6) THE LAND WHERE PHARAOHS RULED- MOSES LED THE PEOPLE OUT OF ___.

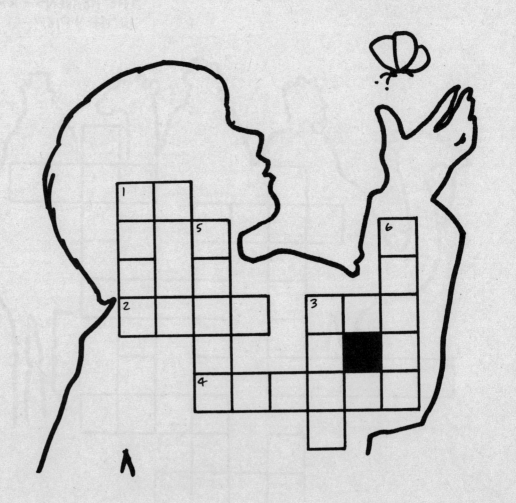

JOHN the BAPTIST

LUKE 3:1-11

ACROSS

1) A DRY, BARREN LAND

2) _____ THE BAPTIST

3) TO TURN AWAY FROM SIN AND DO RIGHT- RHYMES WITH "RESENT"

4) OPPOSITE OF SHE

DOWN

5) JOHN WORE CLOTHES MADE OF ANIMAL _____ (RHYMES WITH "THIN").

6) ONE WHO SPEAKS FOR GOD

7) JOHN ATE LOCUSTS AND WILD _____ (THE SWEET SYRUP BEES MAKE).

JESUS IN THE DESERT

MATTHEW 4:1-11

ACROSS

1) ROCKS

2) SATAN IS THE _____.
   (RHYMES WITH
   "LEVEL")

3) _____ WAS TEMPTED
   IN THE DESERT.

4) SATAN SAID, "IF YOU
   ARE THE SON OF GOD,
   MAKE THESE STONES
   INTO LOAVES OF _____."

DOWN

2) A BARREN, DRY
   LAND

5) THERE IS ONLY _____
   GOD (THE NUMBER
   BEFORE TWO).

6) WICKED, BAD

7) OPPOSITE OF SIT—
   RHYMES WITH
   "HAND"

84

PETER, PHILIP AND NATHANAEL

JOHN 1: 40-51

ACROSS

1) ONES WHO FOLLOW

2) GOD'S DWELLING PLACE ON HIGH

3) MORE THAN ONE MAN - OPPOSITE OF WOMEN

4) OPPOSITE OF OFF

DOWN

1) JESUS NOW HAD _____ FOLLOWERS (THE NUMBER AFTER FOUR).

5) TO PLACE YOUR FAITH IN SOMETHING - "I _____ IN GOD." (RHYMES WITH "RELIEVE")

6) OPPOSITE OF CLOSED

7) A VERY TALL PLANT WITH A TRUNK - RHYMES WITH "FREE"

JESUS CLEANS OUT THE TEMPLE

JOHN 2:12-16

ACROSS

1) THE NUMBER AFTER NINE

2) TO PURCHASE - RHYMES WITH "MY"

3) HOUSE OF WORSHIP

4) OPPOSITE OF BUY

DOWN

1) FLAT PIECES OF FURNITURE ON LEGS- RHYMES WITH "CABLES"

5) WE USE _____ TO BUY THINGS

6) A LION TAMER USES A _____ AND A CHAIR TO CONTROL THE LIONS (RHYMES WITH "RIP")

7) ANGRY

8) OPPOSITE OF IN

HEROD PUTS JOHN IN PRISON

LUKE 3:18-20

ACROSS

1) KING HEROD PUT JOHN THE BAPTIST IN A PRISON FAR _____.

2) OPPOSITE OF LOVED

3) _____ THE BAPTIST

DOWN

2) KING _____ RULED OVER GALILEE.

4) A MAN IS MARRIED TO HIS _____.

5) OPPOSITE OF NO

6) TO USE YOUR BRAIN, MEDITATE - RHYMES WITH "DRINK"

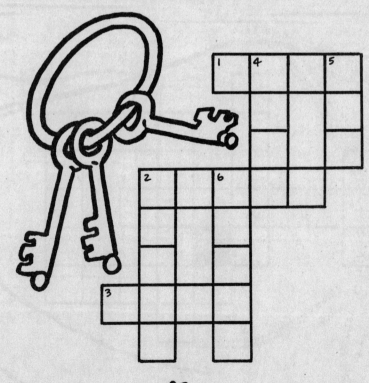

THE NOBLEMAN'S SON

JOHN 4:46-54

ACROSS

1) THERE ARE 24 OF THESE IN ONE DAY, 60 MINUTES IS ONE _____.

2) AN IMPORTANT, RICH MAN OF HIGH RANK

3) THE SON OF GOD

DOWN

1) CURED

4) OPPOSITE OF DAUGHTER, A BOY CHILD

5) WHEN A PERSON IS HOT FROM AN ILLNESS, HE HAS A _____.

6) STREETS, WELL-TRAVELED PATHS - RHYMES WITH "TOADS"

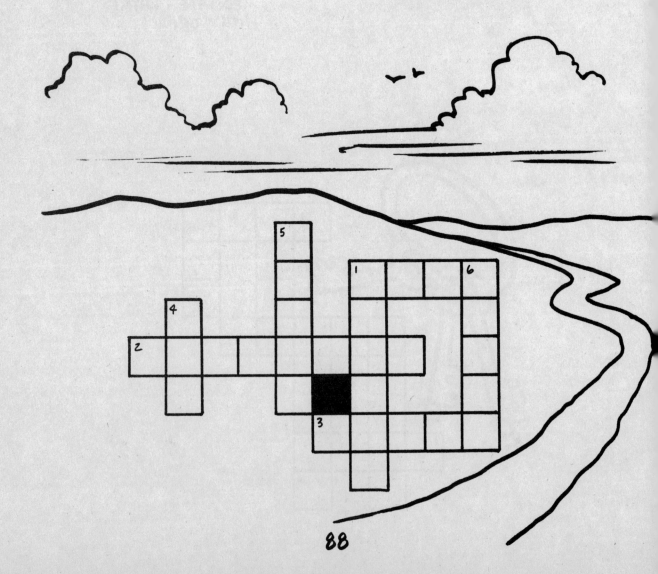

THE FISHERMEN

LUKE 5:1-11

ACROSS

1) A LARGE BODY OF WATER - RHYMES WITH "TEA"

2) A WEB OF CORD FISHERMAN USE TO CATCH FISH - RHYMES WITH "PET"

3) OPPOSITE OF EMPTY

4) VESSELS TO CARRY MEN ON WATER - RHYMES WITH "COATS"

DOWN

3) FINNED CREATURES THAT LIVE IN WATER

5) OPPOSITE OF FEW

6) ONE LESS THAN THREE

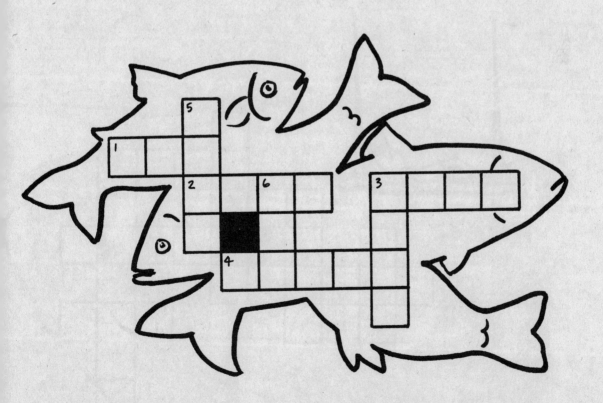

89

THROUGH THE ROOF

ACROSS

1) THE TOP OF A HOUSE

2) AN OWL ASKS, "____?".

3) CURED

4) TO BREAK GOD'S LAW

8) PLACE, LOCATION
   "_____ WERE
   YOU BORN?" -
   RHYMES WITH "HAIR"

DOWN

2) TO STROLL - TRAVEL
   BY FOOT - RHYMES
   WITH "TALK"

5) LARGE GROUP OF
   PEOPLE - RHYMES
   WITH "LOUD"

6) TO PARDON -
   ENDS WITH "GIVE"

7) WE SLEEP IN A ____.

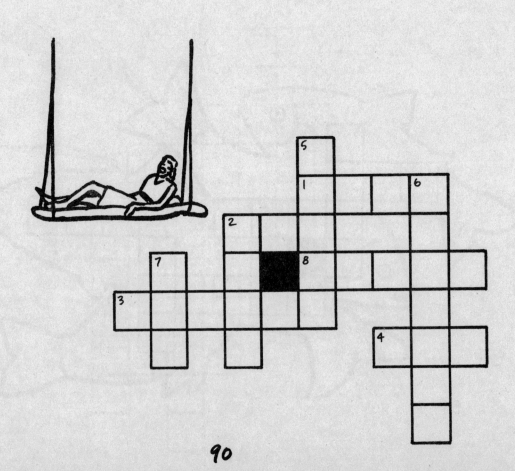

90

JESUS, LORD OF THE SABBATH

MATTHEW 12:1-13

ACROSS

1) OPPOSITE OF SHE

2) THE SEEDS OF CEREAL PLANTS LIKE WHEAT - RHYMES WITH "TRAIN"

3) DEEP HOLE IN THE GROUND - RHYMES WITH "SIT"

4) RULE, STATUTE - RHYMES WITH "PAW"

5) WE HAVE A _____ AT THE END OF EACH ARM.

DOWN

1) WHEN YOU DON'T EAT, YOU GET _____.

6) THE LORD'S DAY, DAY OF REST

7) FARMERS GROW CROPS IN THEIR _____.

8) TO HAVE EATEN - RHYMES WITH "GATE"

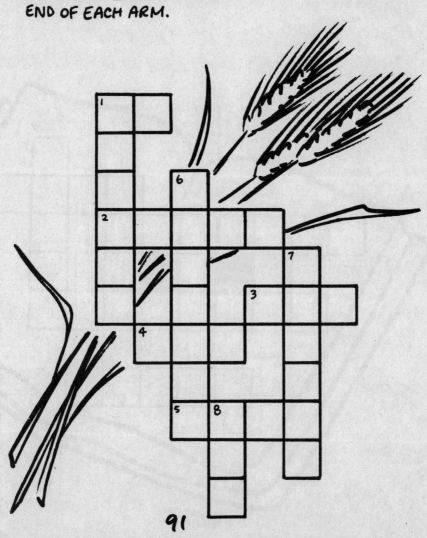

THE TWELVE APOSTLES

LUKE 6:12-16

ACROSS

1) OPPOSITE OF FALSE

2) THE TAX COLLECTOR

3) JESUS CHOSE TWELVE
_____.

4) HIS NAME MEANS
"ROCK"

DOWN

1) THE NUMBER AFTER
ELEVEN

5) OPPOSITE OF BOTTOM

6) OPPOSITE OF HERS
(BELONGING TO HIM)

7) THE APOSTLE WHO
WOULD BETRAY
JESUS.

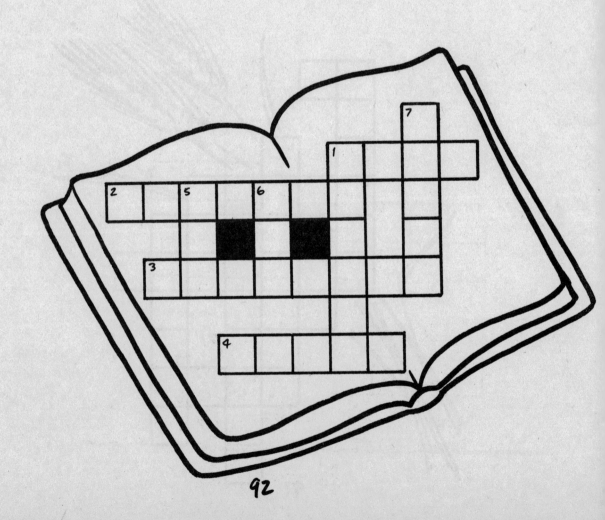

THE SOWER

Luke 8:4-15

ACROSS

1) TO SCATTER SEEDS - RHYMES WITH "TOW"

2) OPPOSITE OF GOOD

3) THE DIRT WE WALK ON, THE EARTH - RHYMES WITH "FOUND"

4) A PLANT GROWS FROM A _____ (RHYMES WITH "FEED").

DOWN

2) WINGED, FEATHERED FLYING CREATURES

3) OPPOSITE OF BAD

5) ROSES HAVE SHARP _____.

6) STONE - RHYMES WITH "CLOCK"

PARABLES OF JESUS

ACROSS

1) STORIES JESUS TOLD TO SHOW A TRUTH

2) RICHES, VALUABLES - "BURIED _____"

3) THE GRAIN WE MAKE FLOUR FROM - RHYMES WITH "SEAT"

4) A PLANT GROWS FROM A _____ (RHYMES WITH "FEED")

DOWN

5) KETCHUP AND _____ GO GREAT ON A HOT DOG (RHYMES WITH "CUSTARD").

6) A BEAUTIFUL FLOWER WITH THORNS - RHYMES WITH "HOSE"

7) WINGED, FEATHERED FLYING CREATURES

8) A VERY TALL PLANT WITH A TRUNK - RHYMES WITH "FREE"

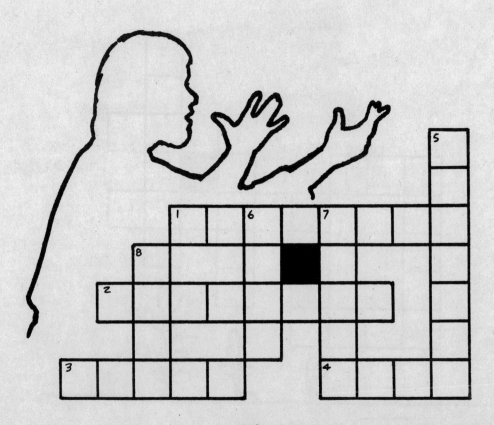

A GIRL LIVES AGAIN

MARK 5:35-43

ACROSS

1) THE GIRL'S PARENTS WERE _____ THAT SHE WAS DEAD (OPPOSITE OF HAPPY).

2) NOT ALIVE

3) TO BE IN THE STATE OF SLEEP

4) OPPOSITE OF FALL — JESUS TOLD THE GIRL TO _____ UP (RHYMES WITH EYES).

DOWN

5) JESUS TOOK HER BY THE _____ (RHYMES WITH "SAND").

6) _____ RAISED THE GIRL FROM THE DEAD.

7) SHE WAS _____ YEARS OLD (ONE MORE THAN ELEVEN).

8) ALL THE PEOPLE MADE A LOUD _____ OUTSIDE (OPPOSITE OF LAUGH).

JESUS WALKS ON WATER
MATTHEW 14:22-27

ACROSS

1) TRAVELED BY FOOT, STROLLED - RHYMES WITH "TALKED"

2) TO BE AFRAID IS TO BE FULL OF _____. (RHYMES WITH "HEAR")

3) A VIOLENT DISTURBANCE IN THE WEATHER - RHYMES WITH "FORM"

DOWN

1) JESUS WALKED ON _____.

4) TRANSPARENT - THE WATER WAS CRYSTAL _____. (RHYMES WITH "FEAR")

5) THE SON OF GOD

6) A VESSEL THAT CARRIES MEN UPON THE WATER - RHYMES WITH "COAT"

JESUS TRANSFIGURED

MARK 9:2-10

ACROSS

1) A TALL PEAK OF LAND

2) GOD SAID, "THIS IS MY BELOVED ____"

3) WHITE FLAKES THAT FALL FROM THE SKY IN WINTER

DOWN

1) THE MAN GOD CHOSE TO LEAD THE PEOPLE OUT OF EGYPT- RHYMES WITH "HOSES"

4) THE DISCIPLE CALLED "THE ROCK"

5) OPPOSITE OF LOW

6) MIDDAY- RHYMES WITH "SOON"

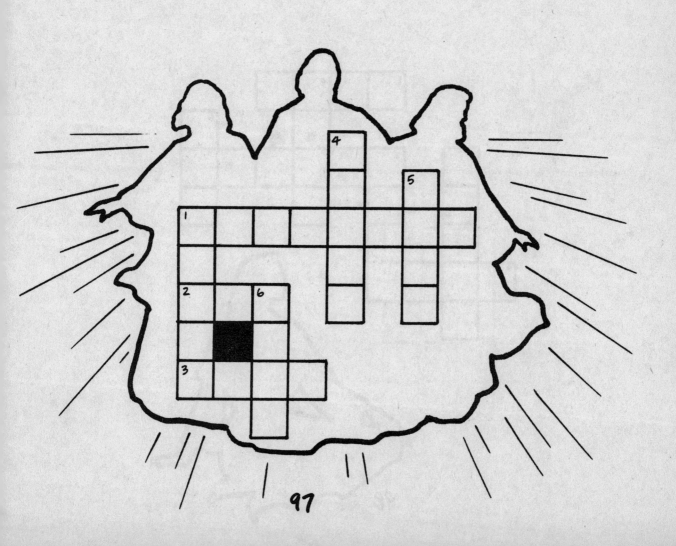

MARY AND MARTHA

LUKE 10:38-42

ACROSS

1) OPPOSITE OF UP

2) _____ WAS TOO BUSY WORKING. (MARY'S SISTER)

3) ACTIVE, DOING MANY THINGS - RHYMES WITH "DIZZY"

DOWN

2) _____ SAT AT THE FEET OF JESUS AND LISTENED TO HIS WORDS. (MARTHA'S SISTER)

4) TO LABOR, EXERT EFFORT- RHYMES WITH "PERK"

5) THE SON OF GOD

6) OPPOSITE OF STAND

ANSWERS

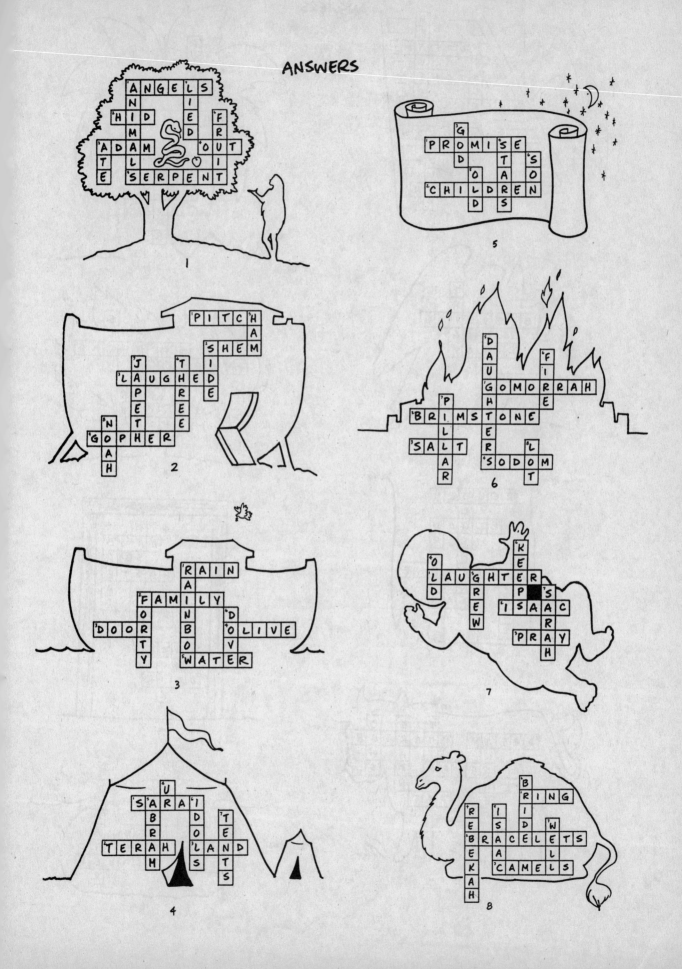

1

ANGELS
N
'HID   'FRUIT
'ADAM   'OUT
'SERPENT

2

'PITCH
'SHEM
'LAUGHED
'J   'TREE
'NOAH
'GOPHER

3

'RAIN
'FAMILY
'DOOR   'OLIVE
'WATER

4

'SARA   'IDOLS   'TENTS
'TERAH   'LAND

5

'PROMISE   'STARS
'CHILDREN

6

'DAUGHTER   'FIRE
'GOMORRAH
'BRIMSTONE
'SALT   'SODOM

7

'LAUGHTER   'KEEP
'ISAAC
'PRAY

8

'BRING
'BRACELETS
'CAMELS

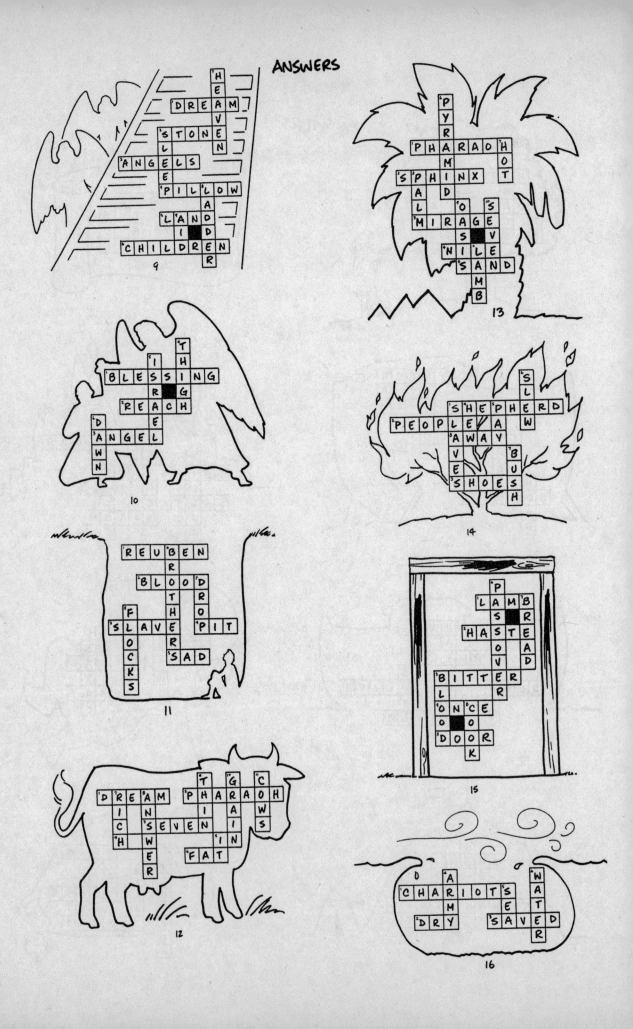

ANSWERS

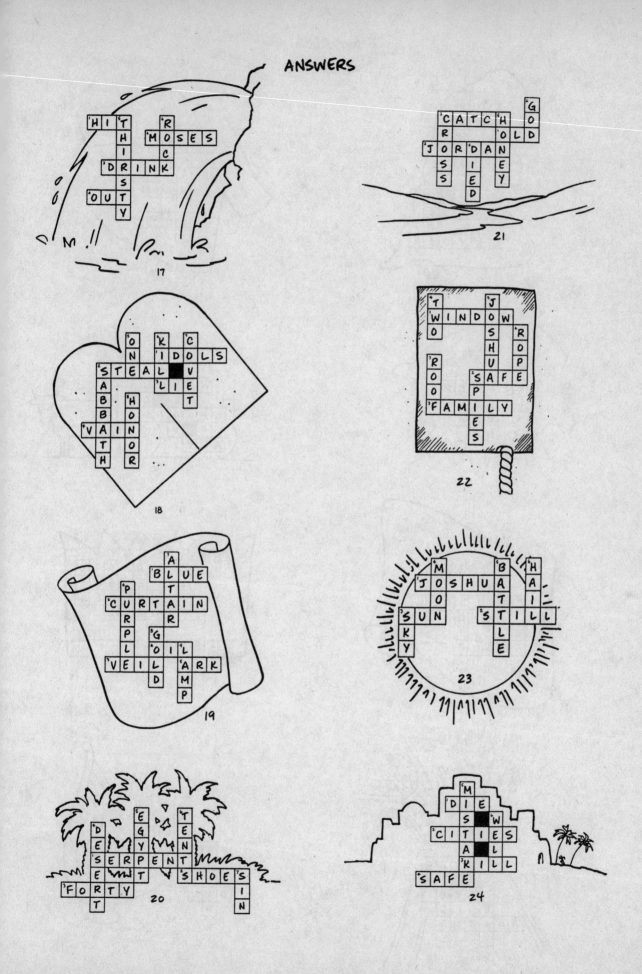

ANSWERS

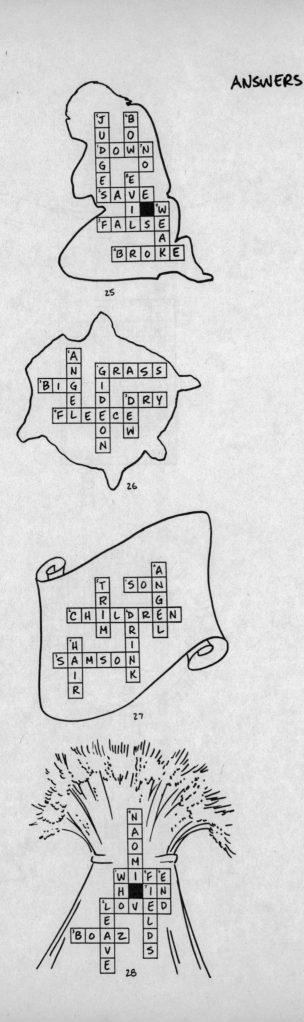

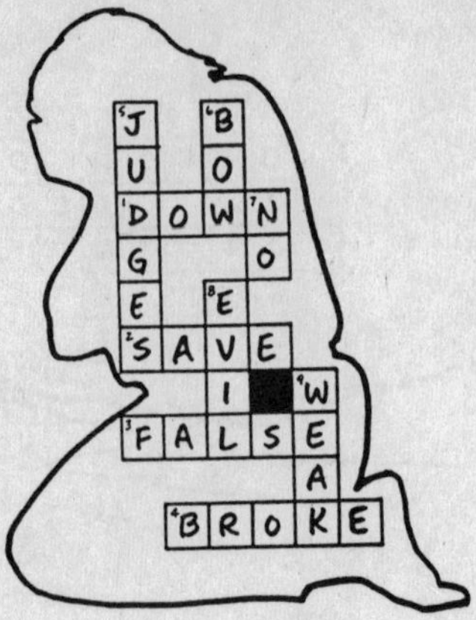
JUDGE
BOW
DOWN
NO
SAVE
FALSE
WEAK
BROKE

25

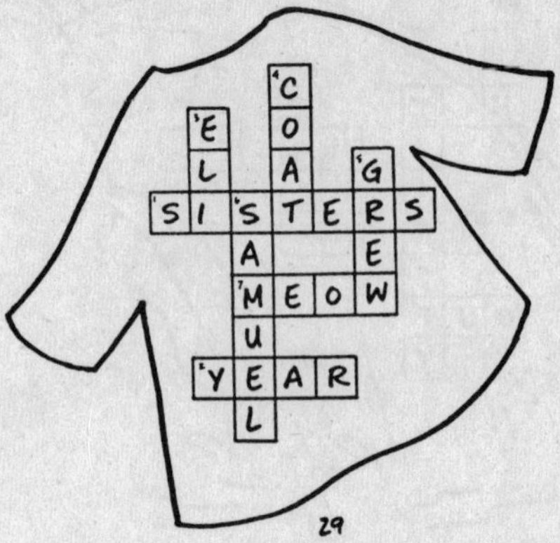
COAT
ELI
GREW
SISTERS
SAMUEL
MEOW
YEAR

29

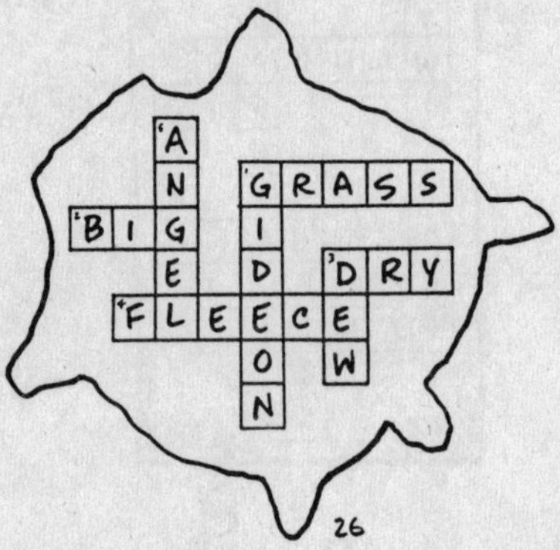
ANGEL
GRASS
BIG
GIDEON
DRY
FLEECE
DEW

26

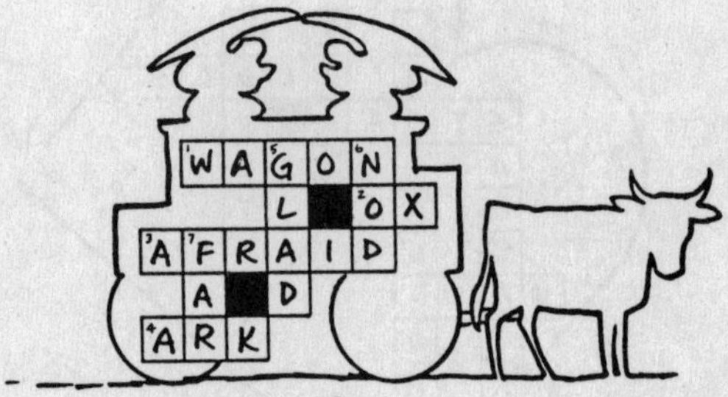
WAGON
OX
AFRAID
ARK

30

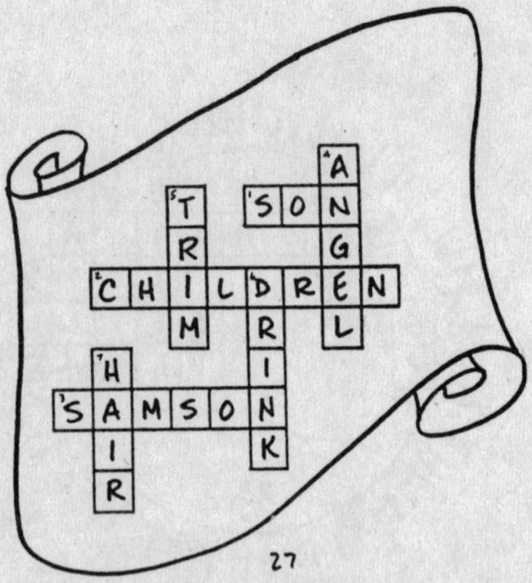
ANGEL
SON
TRIM
CHILDREN
DRINK
HAIR
SAMSON

27

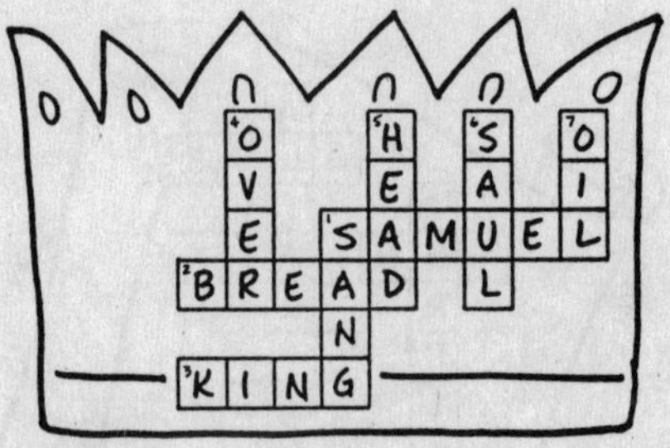
OVER
HEAD
SAUL
OIL
SAMUEL
BREAD
KING

31

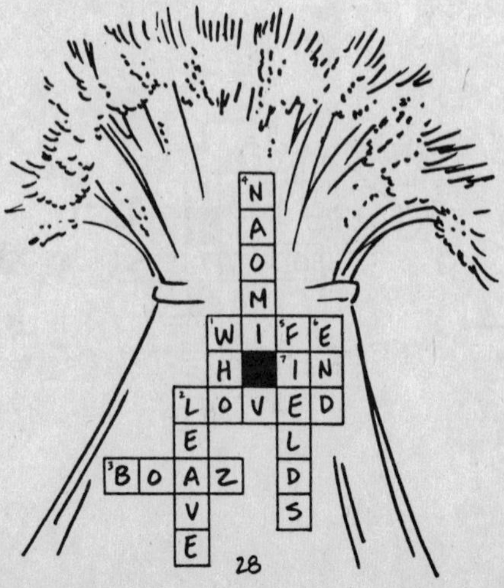
NAOMI
WIFE
WHO
FIELDS
IN
LOVED
LEAVE
BOAZ

28

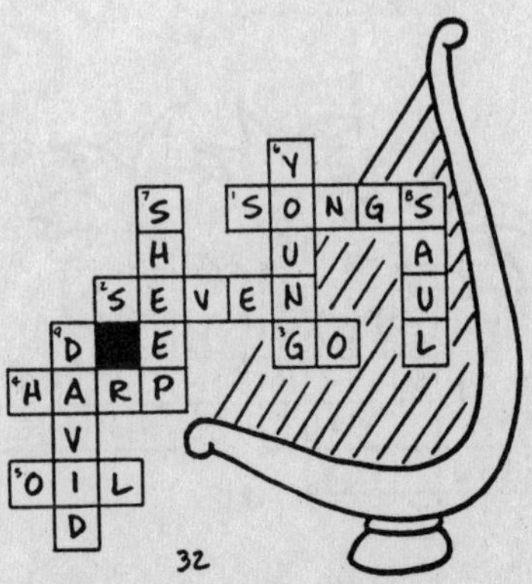
YOUNG
SONG
SHEEP
SAUL
SEVEN
GO
DAVID
HARP
OIL

32

ANSWERS

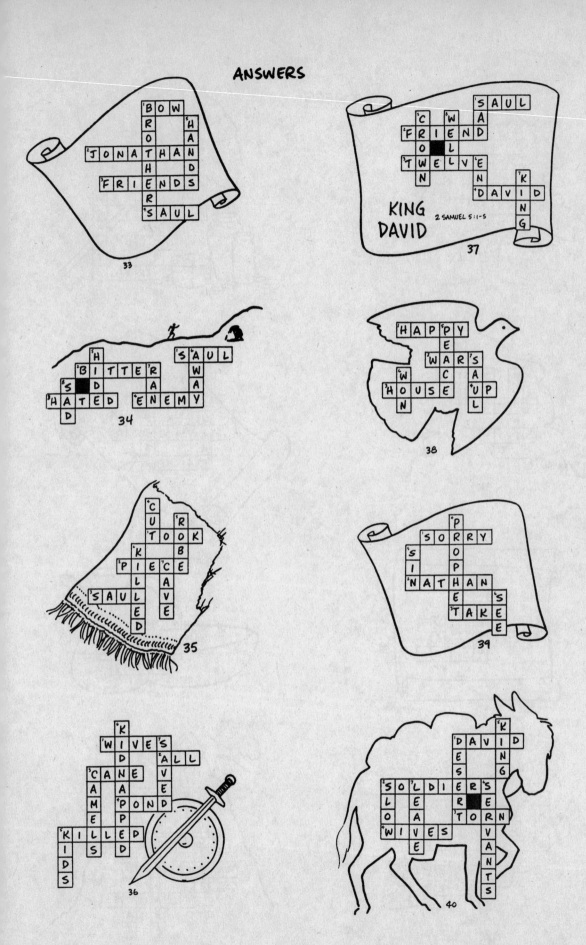

33
- BOW
- BROTHER
- HAND / HANDS
- JONATHAN
- FRIENDS
- SAUL

37
- SAUL
- SAD
- CROWN
- WOLVEN
- FRIEND
- TWELVE
- DAVID
- KING

KING DAVID — 2 SAMUEL 5:1-5

34
- HD
- BITTER
- SAUL
- RA
- WAY
- SAD
- HATED
- ENEMY

38
- HAPPY
- PEACE
- WAR'S
- WON
- HOUSE
- SAUL
- UP

35
- CUT
- TOOK
- ROB
- KILLED
- PIECE
- CAVE
- SAUL

39
- PROP
- SORRY
- SIN
- NATHAN
- PEOPLE
- TAKE
- SEE

36
- KID
- WIVES
- ALL
- CANE
- AVE
- CAMELS
- POND
- APPED
- KILLED
- KIDS

40
- KING
- DAVID
- DESERT
- SOLDIER'S
- SLOAN
- EVER
- TORN
- WIVES
- SERVANTS

ANSWERS

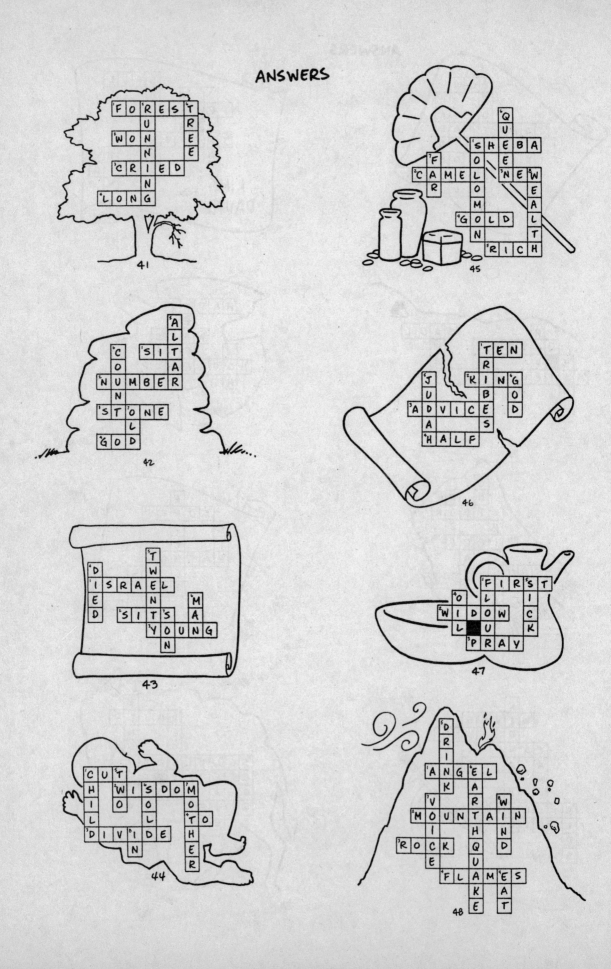

ANSWERS

49

B¹E D ²V ⁴B A D
L I ³K I L L E D A
I N D
J A²J E Z E B E L
A H ⁵F A M I L Y
⁶D O G S

53

¹F E L L
²F L
³W O O D
⁴I N T O⁵O
A U
⁶W A T E R
X

50

¹G I V E ²S ³M E N
R W O
O ⁴S E N
U ⁵W A T E R
N L T
⁶D E A T H

54

¹F O U R
O
²G O N E
D ³M E N
P
⁴N P⁵T E N T S
⁶M O N E Y E
I E⁷S E E W

51

²A
L
³S I C K
I
⁴F A T H E R
⁵B E E
⁶L O V E⁷D
Y ⁸T I E
D

55

¹L I O N S
D ⁴P
²C O U N T R I E S
L I
³S T R E E T S
S
⁵C I T Y

52

²C
O
³H E N
⁴M A N
¹B R E A D Y
T
⁵P L E N T Y
A
⁶T A L K

56

²S ⁴T
¹L I V E ⁵A S K
I E H ⁶P
C A A R
K R ⁷S U N D I A L
O
⁸D O W N

ANSWERS

57

BAD / KILLED / IDOLS / SINNED / NUN / MOON

61

GUELDAD / BELT / CRIED / SI / STONES / FIRST

58

HEART / SONGS / THANKS / JEHOSHAPHAT / PARA / KINGS / KEY

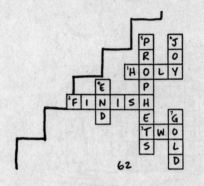

62

PROPHETS / JOY / HOLY / E / FINISH / TWO / GOLD

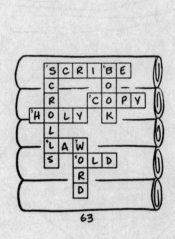

59

TEMPLE / SEVEN / REPAIR / NEW / WOOD / BOX

63

SCRIBE / SCROLLS / BOOK / COPY / HOLY / LAW / WORD / OLD

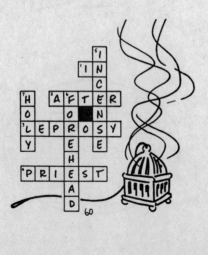

60

INCENSE / HOLY / AFTER / LEPROSY / OVERHEAD / PRIEST

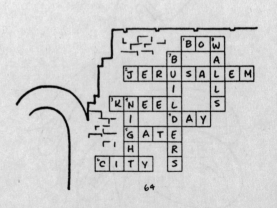

64

BOW / WALLS / BUILD / JERUSALEM / KNEEL / DAY / LIGHT / GATE / ERS / CITY

Puzzle 65 — scroll crossword:
PULL
HAPPY / PEOPLE / PULL / UP / R
PROMISE / REST
EZRA

65

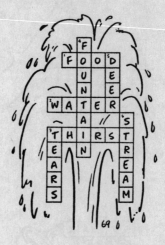

Puzzle 69 — fountain crossword:
FOOD / DEER
FOUNTAIN
WATER / R
TEARS / THIRST / STREAM

69

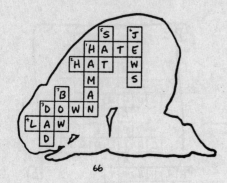

Puzzle 66 — rock crossword:
S / J
HATE / EWS
HAT / M / W
B / A
DOWN / N
LAW / D

66

Puzzle 70 — music notes crossword:
K / HIS / I / N
F / LORD / D
HIM / N / R / E
TRUTH / PRAISE / E / S
FOREVER / S
HONOR

70

Puzzle 67 — dinner/cup crossword:
E / SAVED / D
STHER / I
HAMAN / N
HER / JEWS / E / R

67

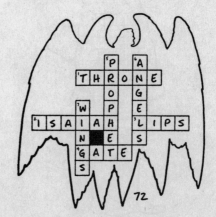

Puzzle 71 — rose crossword:
WORK'S / T
WOMAN / R
ARMS / GOOD / O
HOUSE / HANDS / N / G
HUSBAND

71

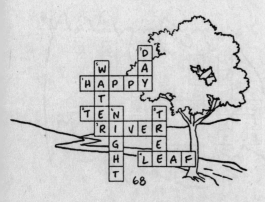

Puzzle 68 — tree/river crossword:
DAY
WATER
HAPPY
TE / N / TREE
RIVER / I / R
NIGHT / LEAF / G / H / T

68

Puzzle 72 — wings crossword:
P / A
THRONE / N
O / G
W / P / E / LIPS
ISAIAH / E / S
N / GATE / G / S

72

ANSWERS

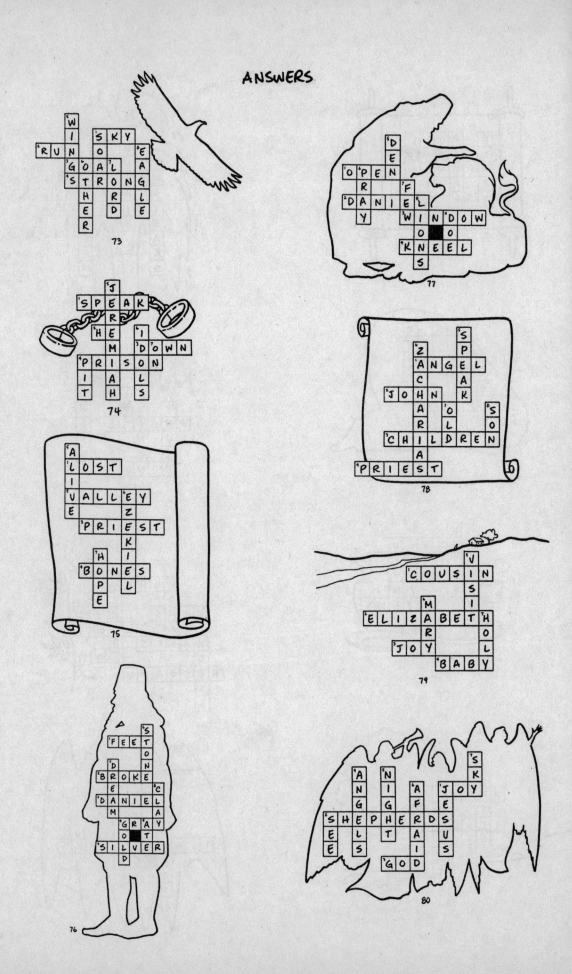

73

W I N
S K Y
R U N O A E A
G O A L G A
S T R O N G L
H R E
E D
R

74

J
S P E A K
E R
H E I
D O W N
P R I S O N
I T A L
H S

75

A
L O S T
I
V A L L E Y
E Z
P R I E S T
K
H I
B O N E S
P L
E

76

S
F E E T T
D O
B R O K E N
E C
D A N I E L A
E L
G R A Y Y
O T
S I L V E R D

77

D
O P E N
R F
D A N I E L
Y W I N D O W
O O
K N E E L
S

78

S
Z P
A N G E L E
C A
J O H N K
H O
A S
R L O
C H I L D R E N
A N
P R I E S T

79

V
C O U S I N
S
M I
E L I Z A B E T H
R O
J O Y L
B A B Y

80

S
A N A J O Y
N I F E
S H E P H E R D S
E G R U
E H A S
L I D
S G O D
T

ANSWERS

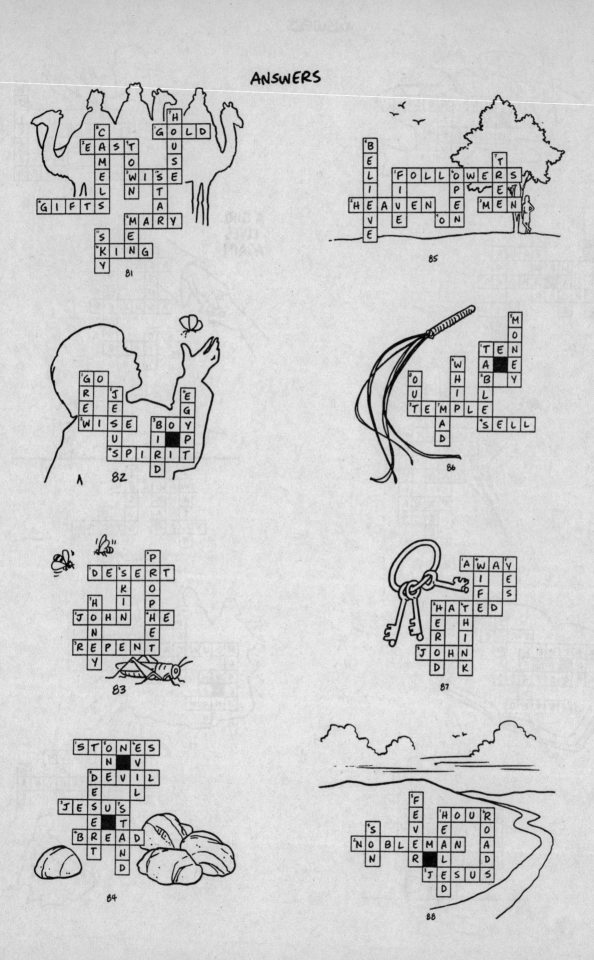

81

Across/Down: CAMEL, EAST, TOWN, WISE, HOUSE, GOLD, STAR, GIFTS, MARY, KING, SKY

85

BELIEVE, FOLLOWERS, OPEN, TREE, HEAVEN, MEN, ON

82

GO, GREW, JESUS, WISE, EGYPT, BOY, SPIRIT

86

MONEY, TEN, TABLE, WHIP, OUT, TEMPLE, SELL

83

DESERT, PROPHET, KING, HONEY, JOHN, REPENT

87

AWAY, WIFE, YES, HATED, HEROD, THINK, JOHN

84

STONES, DEVIL, JESUS, STAND, BREAD

88

FEVER, HOUR, ROAD, NOBLEMAN, SON, HERALD, JESUS

ANSWERS

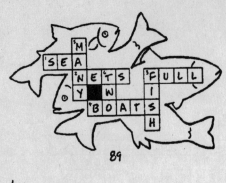

89

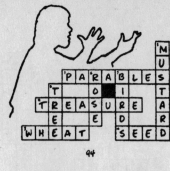

94

A GIRL
LIVES
AGAIN

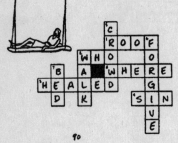

90

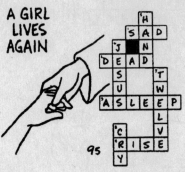

95

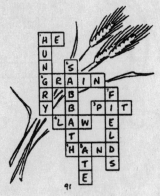

91

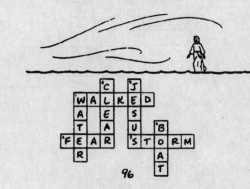

96

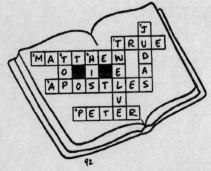

92

97

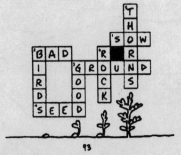

93

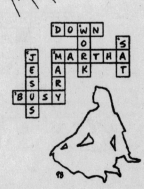

98